Wagner's *Ring* in 18

Studies in German Literature, Linguistics, and Culture

Wagner's *Ring* in 1848

New Translations of
The Nibelung Myth and *Siegfried's Death*

Translated and with an introduction by
Edward R. Haymes

ch CAMDEN HOUSE

Rochester, New York

First published 2010 by Camden House
Transferred to digital printing 2013
Reprinted in paperback 2015

Camden House is an imprint of Boydell & Brewer Inc.
668 Mt. Hope Avenue, Rochester, NY 14620, USA
www.camden-house.com
and of Boydell & Brewer Limited
PO Box 9, Woodbridge, Suffolk IP12 3DF, UK
www.boydellandbrewer.com

Paperback ISBN-13: 978-1-57113-932-0
Paperback ISBN-10: 1-57113-932-X
Hardcover ISBN-13: 978-1-57113-379-3
Hardcover ISBN-10: 1-57113-379-8

Library of Congress Cataloging-in-Publication Data

Wagner, Richard, 1813-1883.
    [Nibelungen-Mythus als Entwurf zu einem Drama. English &
German]
    Wagner's Ring in 1848: new translations of the Nibelung myth and
Siegfried's death / translated and with an introduction by Edward R.
Haymes.
        p. cm. — (Studies in German literature, linguistics, and culture)
Includes bibliographical references and index.
ISBN-13: 978-1-57113-379-3 (hardcover: alk. paper)
ISBN-10: 1-57113-379-8 (hardcover: alk. paper)
    1. Wagner, Richard, 1813–1883. Ring des Nibelungen—Sources.
2. Opera—Germany—19th century—Sources. I. Haymes, Edward,
1940– II. Title. III. Series.

ML410.W15W1213 2010
782.1—dc22

                                                          2010006566

This publication is printed on acid-free paper.
Printed in the United States of America.

Contents

Preface

THE PRINCIPAL REASON for the current volume is to provide modern
translations of the two texts included: Wagner's draft, which he called
"Der Nibelungen Mythus als Entwurf zu einem Drama" and the verse
libretto *Siegfried's Tod*, which was eventually revised to become *Götterdämmerung* in the great cycle *Der Ring des Nibelungen*. Since it would be
inappropriate to present these texts without discussing how they came
about, I have included an overview of the major developments toward an
understanding of the Nibelung legend in Germany in the first half of the
nineteenth century. I have also included an examination of the influence of
the much-maligned *Nibelungenlied* on the final shape of the *Ring*. Finally I
have attempted to show how the translated texts relate to the version of the
Ring cycle we know today.

I have not attempted to recapitulate Wagner's life up to this point or to
interpret the final form of the cycle, but rather to present what we have of
Wagner's plan to compose a single opera on the Nibelung legend, which he
put on paper in the fall of 1848. This is certainly not an exploration of the
political events of that fateful year, nor of Wagner's part in those events.
These areas are far better covered elsewhere. I have included a number of
titles in my suggestions for further reading that address these points from the
point of view of the biographer and the musicologist.

I am very grateful to the many people who have encouraged me along
the way. I am particularly grateful to Barry Millington, who read my translation of *Siegfried's Death* and made a number of helpful suggestions before
deciding that it and the accompanying commentary were too large to include in the *Wagner Journal*, to which I had originally submitted them. I am
also grateful to the anonymous reviewers engaged by Camden House, who
pointed out shortcomings and errors in my discussion and translation. They
were particularly useful in pointing out the musicological problems that had
arisen because I am a Germanist and thus not a member of their guild. They
also helped me locate some things that had been lost in the Wagnerian fog
surrounding the works. I would like to thank the librarians and curators of
special collections at the Staatsbibliothek Preußischer Kulturbesitz in Berlin,
the Morgan Library in New York, the Cleveland Public Library, and the
Michael Schwartz Library at Cleveland State University for making the many
texts cited here available. Many titles would have been unavailable to me if
they had not been scanned by Google Books. I am grateful to Cleveland

State University for its program of Professional Leaves of Absence that allowed me to carry out research in Berlin during the winter of 2009. Finally I would like to commend James Walker for his patience and his readiness to work with me through the process of producing this book.

Edward R. Haymes
October 19, 2009

Introduction: Wagner's Nibelungs in 1848

On the Eve of Two Revolutions

IN THE SUMMER AND FALL of 1848 Richard Wagner stood on the brink of
two revolutions, one of which seemed to him and his contemporaries far
more momentous than the other.[1] History has judged otherwise. The political
revolution that would, in a few months, sweep Wagner into its toils and leave
him a wanted fugitive was ultimately only one in a series of attempts to unify
Germany and move toward something other than a collection of tiny states
under aristocratic absolutism.[2] The unification movement took another twenty-
odd years and ended with a compromise that would never have satisfied such
young revolutionaries as Richard Wagner, August Röckel, or the "anarchist
from outside," Mikhail Bakunin. At the same time, Wagner was moving toward a musical and dramatic revolution that he associated with the political,
but which would change the musical and operatic landscape forever. Operas
composed in the twentieth and even the twenty-first century are still poised on
the border between music and drama that Wagner defined in his theoretical
writings of the following five years. The composer's role in both revolutions
has been explored ad nauseam, but the situation of the Nibelung legend just
before it blossomed out into Wagner's monumental tetralogy has only been
touched upon.

In 1848 Wagner was thirty-five years old and had composed six of his
thirteen operas (only three of which the composer recognized as belonging to
the "Wagner canon"). Three (*Rienzi, Der fliegende Holländer,* and *Tannhäuser*) had been performed in Dresden, where he was *Kapellmeister* (i.e. one

---

[1] For a far more detailed description of Wagner's last months in Dresden and his flight
to Zurich, see Martin Gregor-Dellin, *Richard Wagner: Sein Leben, Sein Werk, Sein
Jahrhundert* (Munich: Goldmann, 1983), 245–76. Gregor-Dellin manages to construct
a detailed description of Wagner's participation in the uprising, which Wagner played
down in his own writings. An abridged English translation by J. Maxwell Brownjohn is
Richard Wagner: His Life, His Work, His Century (San Diego, New York, London:
Harcourt Brace Jovanovich, 1983), 152–82. A short overview of this period is contained in Barry Millington, *Wagner* (Princeton: Princeton UP, 1992), 33–40.

[2] The history of Germany during this period has been treated in numerous studies. The
English-speaking reader will find useful the study by Mike Rapport, *1848: Year of
Revolution* (New York: Basic Books, 2008), and the literature cited there.

of two conductors with administrative duties) at the Royal Court Theater. *Lohengrin,* which had been completed earlier in 1848, had been rejected for performance in Dresden and was awaiting a premiere. He was becoming increasingly disaffected with his situation in Dresden and sought an outlet for his energies in politics, a move that in a few months would spell the end of his time in Dresden and of his tenure as royal *Kapellmeister.*

It is impossible to determine when the idea of writing an opera on the Nibelung legend first entered Wagner's mind. Like most nationalistic Germans of his time, he had been drawn to the material because of its importance to "Germanic" culture, but — as we shall see — he was unhappy with its most famous incarnation, the Middle High German *Nibelungenlied.* As he became acquainted with the Icelandic poetry and prose of the *Eddas,* the prose of the *Völsungasaga,* and the Norwegian prose of the *Thidrekssaga,* he found a different version of the same story, one in which Siegfried played a more extensive role and one that he felt was closer to the mythic thrust of the "original."

Der Ring des Nibelungen (*The Ring of the Nibelung*) is one of the most ambitious works of art ever attempted. It is certainly the largest work regularly performed on the stage today. If one does not try to account for the reading that Wagner did leading up to his writing of it, it was begun in 1848 and not completed until November of 1874, when the composer penned the last notes of *Götterdämmerung. Der Ring des Nibelungen* was first performed as a cycle in the Bayreuth *Festspielhaus* in the summer of 1876.[3] If we want to understand Wagner's creative process as well as his attitude toward myth, history, and politics, we must look at the operatic project he settled on in the last few months before the uprising in Dresden that cost him his position and almost his life. The *Ring* cycle has been the object of dozens of books and hundreds of articles attempting to analyze every aspect of the work. This little book is not designed to add to that mass of interpretation, but to provide a point of departure. It is a commonplace of Wagner biography that the composer set out to write a single Nibelung opera, *Siegfried's Tod*[4] (*Siegfried's Death*), and that he expanded his ideas backward over the years following his exile from Dresden. He did, however, think enough of this first attempt at a Nibelung drama to include it in his *Gesammelte Schriften und Dichtungen* (*Collected Writings and Poetry*), published in 1870.[5] This study is built around a new

---

[3] *Das Rheingold* was first performed in 1869 and *Die Walküre* in 1870 in Munich, both against the composer's wishes. King Ludwig II of Bavaria demanded these performances, which he had every right to do, since Wagner had exchanged the scores of (and the rights to) these works for the king's financial support.

[4] Wagner included an apostrophe in the German title of the opera, although most modern citations refer to it in the current German style as *Siegfrieds Tod.*

[5] All quotes from Wagner's prose works and *Siegfried's Tod* are from the edition: Richard Wagner, *Sämtliche Schriften und Dichtungen,* 16 vols. (Leipzig: Breitkopf und

translation of *Siegfried's Tod,* which has languished in an impenetrable translation made by William Ashton Ellis and published in 1899. Wagner had, however, already sketched out a conception of the Nibelung myth that went far beyond the events included in the libretto for *Siegfried's Tod.* He also published this text in his *Gesammelte Schriften und Dichtungen* under the title "Der Nibelungen-Mythus als Entwurf zu einem Drama." I have supplied a new translation of this text as well.

Several relatively recent studies have provided a great deal of information on the sources that led to the eventual cycle. Without going back to Wolfgang Golther's and Hermann Schneider's explorations of Wagner's use of his medieval sources,[6] we can recognize three recent studies that contribute greatly to our understanding of the evolution of the *Ring* out of the Nibelung fog that surrounded the topic in the 1840s. The first of these is the fragment left behind by Deryck Cooke at his death, which would eventually be published under the title *I Saw the World End.*[7] Cooke not only identified the medieval sources of much of Wagner's myth, but also informed us to a large extent what editions and translations Wagner had used to arrive at his work. Presumably Cooke would have treated the transformation from *Siegfried's Tod* to *Götterdämmerung* if he had gotten that far in his analysis. A second study, which concentrates on Wagner's sources, his reading, and his own books, is Elizabeth Magee's *Richard Wagner and the Nibelungs,* published in 1990.[8] Magee has done yeoman work in exploring the books in Wagner's personal library in Dresden and the works that he borrowed from the Saxon Royal Library that may have contributed to his concept. She also makes a good case for his knowledge of several works that fall into neither category. A third book, by the Icelander Árni Björnsson, has been translated into English under the title *Wagner and the Volsungs.*[9] This work is animated by the author's desire to see Snorri's *Edda,* the *Poetic Edda,* and the *Völsungasaga* correctly identified as

---

Härtel, n.d. [1911]). This is one of many reprints of Wagner's works made after the original publication of the ten-volume *Gesammelte Schriften und Dichtungen* under Wagner's direction during the period from 1871 to 1883. Quotes from the *Ring* are from Stewart Spencer's translation in *Wagner's Ring of the Nibelung: A Companion,* ed. Stewart Spencer and Barry Millington (New York: Thames and Hudson, 1993).

[6] Wolfgang Golther, *Die sagengeschichtlichen Grundlagen der Ringdichtung Richard Wagners* (Berlin: Lehsten, 1902); Hermann Schneider, "Richard Wagner und das germanische Altertum," *Kleine Schriften* (Berlin: de Gruyter, 1962), 107–24.

[7] Deryck Cooke, *I Saw the World End: A Study of Wagner's* Ring (Oxford: Oxford UP, 1979).

[8] Elizabeth Magee, *Richard Wagner and the Nibelungs* (Oxford: Clarendon Press, 1990).

[9] Árni Björnsson, *Wagner and the Volsungs: Icelandic Sources of* Der Ring des Nibelungen, trans. Anthony Faulkes and Anna Yates (London: Viking Society for Northern Research, 2003).

the products of his home culture, the unique literary world of Iceland in the thirteenth century. He sees the identification of these works with the Germanic past as a danger to the recognition of their specifically Icelandic nature. He may be right about modern understandings of the Icelandic texts, but it would be a mistake to think that Wagner and his generation saw the Norse materials as anything other than poetry from the Germanic past. Árni Björnsson does, however, provide a valuable overview of the Icelandic sources for practically every line of the text.

Elizabeth Magee has done a commendable job of describing Wagner's reading and the influences that we find in the "Nibelungen-Mythus," which was written in early October 1848, and in the first verse version of *Siegfried's Tod*, written in November of the same year. She argues that Wagner did not see the *Völsungasaga* until after he completed the "Nibelungen-Mythus," that is, late October 1848.[10] She traces the elements of the scenario that seem to derive directly from the saga to retellings in the secondary literature to which Wagner had access. It may never be possible to tie down every motif of the plot by reference to some source; however, it is clear from Wagner's discussions that he thought of the Nibelung story as a mythic whole and shaped it to make sense as drama on the stage. I have an image of Wagner soaking in every bit of the Nibelung atmosphere that was available and then gradually forming it in his mind into a story that made sense to him. The Icelandic versions of the story allowed him to see the mythical structure of the whole, a structure that had been hidden from him as long as he knew only the version in the *Nibelungenlied*. He outlined this development several years after starting on the project in his autobiographical sketch *Eine Mitteilung an meine Freunde* (A Communication to My Friends, 1851):

> Even if the magnificent figure of Siegfried had always attracted me, it first really enchanted me when I was successful in seeing it freed of all later costuming in its purest human appearance before me. Only now did I recognize the possibility of making him the hero of a drama; something that had never occurred to me as long as I only knew him from the medieval Nibelungenlied.[11]

These remarks were made in the context of Wagner's discussion of his rejection of historical drama in favor of myth, which he understood as the product

---

[10] Magee, *Richard Wagner and the Nibelungs*, 44–46.

[11] "Hatte mich nun schon längst die herrliche Gestalt des Siegfried angezogen, so entzückte sie mich doch vollends erst, als es mir gelungen war, sie, von aller späteren Umkleidung befreit, in ihrer reinsten menschlichen Erscheinung vor mir zu sehen. Erst jetzt auch erkannte ich die Möglichkeit, ihn zum Helden eines Drama's zu machen, was mir nie eingefallen war, so lange ich ihn nur aus dem mittelalterlichen Nibelungenliede kannte." Wagner, *Sämtliche Schriften und Dichtungen*, 4:312.

of the *Volk,* the whole people.[12] Note his use of the term "medieval" as a pejorative. Like most of his contemporaries he felt that the Icelandic texts represented a far earlier, more "primitive" version of the Nibelung legend, one that was far closer to the mythic roots of the story, than the "medieval" *Nibelungenlied.* Again, like most scholars at the time, Wagner ignored the fact that the Norse versions known to him may have been as much affected by the Icelandic world from which they emerged as the *Nibelungenlied* was by its high medieval German surroundings. They were certainly written down somewhat later than the Middle High German epic, most datings placing them in the middle to the second half of the thirteenth century, while the epic is dated around 1200.

As we read these excellent studies, we must keep in mind the fact that they all assume the completed *Ring* poem as a basis. I have attempted to work the other way and to approach the construction of the *Ring* myth as a project Wagner worked out in the late 1840s and presented for the first time in these texts. He thought they were important enough to include in his collected writings and, except for the few mentions in his letters and other writings, they are the best indication available to us today of his thinking at the time. Readers of Wagner's own words in his autobiography, *Mein Leben,* or of any of the other primary sources must keep in mind that he was presenting himself to an audience: a king, or a second wife, who would judge him on the basis of that depiction. We must also keep in mind that he was recalling events at a distance of many years.

Wagner attempted to set some of his text to music sometime before 1850, but he was apparently unable to find a musical language that would suit the new project.[13] He needed the theoretical underpinnings he would work out in the pages of *Oper und Drama,* the most important of his theoretical writings from the early Zurich period. Even with the new theoretical musings it took him several years to achieve most of the textual changes that would later find their way into the *Ring of the Nibelung.* He realized that the backstory of his Siegfried opera was simply too large to be included in the backward-looking

---

[12] In a recent article, Barry Millington has explored the turbulent world of creative ideas that Wagner entertained along with his work on the Nibelung legend, which, however, eventually became the center of his creative work. "After the Revolution: The *Ring* in the Light of Wagner's Dresden and Zurich Projects," *University of Toronto Quarterly* 74 (2005): 676–92.

[13] Robert Bailey transcribed the musical sketches associated with *Siegfried's Tod* and examined their musical and literary lineage in an article titled "Wagner's Musical Sketches for *Siegfrieds Tod,*" in *Studies in Music History: Essays for Oliver Strunk,* ed. Harold Powers (Princeton: Princeton UP, 1968), 459–94. A sample of this music as realized by Werner Breig can be heard on the disc *Richard Wagner im Schweizer Exil,* MG CD 6156, published by the Migros-Genossenschafts-Bund in Zurich in 1999.

passages in *Siegfried's Tod,* and he attempted to clarify things in 1850 with a second opera dealing with Siegfried's youth. He called this opera *Der junge Siegfried* (*Young Siegfried*). Finally he realized the need for additional prequels and wrote the scenario and then the poetic texts for *Die Walküre* and *Das Rheingold.* When these texts were completed, he went back and revised his earlier work to agree with them, publishing the revised text of the *Ring* cycle (still without this name) in 1853 in a private printing for his friends.[14] He began work on the mammoth composition of the music in November 1853. He retained the titles *Der junge Siegfried* and *Siegfried's Tod* for the last two operas of the cycle until 1856, when he switched to *Siegfried* and *Götterdämmerung.* He brought all four works together under their present titles and published them with an introduction in 1863.

The Aims and Approaches of This Book

A balanced discussion of Wagner's treatment of the Nibelung myth has to look in both directions. We cannot read his early sketches today without thinking of what became of them. For this reason, in the facing-page original German text of *Siegfried's Tod* provided here, I have italicized all the lines that survived into the last opera of his giant cycle, eventually renamed *Götterdämmerung.* Wagner already added the passage we know as Hagen's Watch in February of 1849[15] and made many attempts at refashioning Brünnhilde's final scene.[16] The final version of the published text even contains a passage that was not included in the musical setting of the drama, so we know that he was unsatisfied with the conclusion throughout the process of composition. There are numerous studies of this process, but they pick up the story after the artificial limit I have set myself here: December 31, 1848.

It is clear that Wagner judged that only minimal editorial preparation of the texts was necessary, since he generally entrusted the task to other hands, including those of the young professor from Basel, Friedrich Nietzsche. The

---

[14] Wagner never intended this printing to be available to anyone but his closest friends. Two copies, however, have found their way into the Morgan Library in New York. The more important of these contains Wagner's own corrections as he worked toward a final version.

[15] He may have added it earlier. Warren Darcy maintains that this revision of *Siegfried's Tod* was actually produced before December 18, 1848, which would place it in the time frame of this study, but this early version has been lost. Thus the earliest version of this scene was not added until February 1849. Warren Darcy, *Wagner's Das Rheingold* (Oxford: Clarendon Press, 1993), 9.

[16] All of the surviving texts of this scene are included in Spencer's translation contained in *Wagner's Ring of the Nibelung: A Companion,* ed. Stewart Spencer and Barry Millington (New York: Thames and Hudson, 1993), 360–63.

preparation Wagner demanded can be found mainly in the spelling changes he had made since drafting the early documents. Wagner used the spelling "Wodan" until fairly late (including in the text of the opera *Lohengrin*), but his musical ear demanded that it be changed to "Wotan"; to reflect this, the text of *Siegfried's Tod* was changed prior to publication in his *Gesammelte Schriften*, the preparation of which began in 1870, but the spelling of Gunther's sister's name remains "Gudrune" in this text rather than the "Gutrune" of the final version. This is clearly not an area where we can seek consistency, nor is it something to which we can attach great importance.[17] For my translation I have used the versions of both texts Wagner saw fit to publish in his *Gesammelte Schriften*. Both texts underwent some revision at various times, but Warren Darcy has established that the text of *Siegfried's Tod* is essentially that completed in December 1848 (as prepared for publication by Friedrich Nietzsche) and the "Nibelung-Mythus" text in the *Gesammelte Schriften* was made from a copy made from the original, not from the revised fair copy, so that it too represents a quite early version of the text.[18] It would be far too complicated to review all the revisions that were made in both texts, and this information is available elsewhere in musicological sources.[19] Suffice it to say that the versions published in the *Gesammelte Schriften* are sufficiently early to represent Wagner's thoughts on the *Ring* in 1848, which is the topic at hand in the present volume.

Along with the translations of Wagner's texts, I have attempted to collect a few materials that complement them. I provide as part of this introduction an overview of the Nibelung legend in Germany in the first half of the nineteenth century as it would have been known to an educated German. Since it has been neglected in deference to Wagner's own remarks, I have explored the influence of the *Nibelungenlied* on the poem. Finally, I have included after the translation a sketch of the changes Wagner made in using these documents as the basis of his final poem for the *Ring*. Since this book is designed for the English-speaking reader, I have given sources in English general preference, but a large portion of the sources available to me are available only in German. In order to make this introduction as useful as possible, I have also included these sources in the footnotes. With some exceptions, I have included those books that are available in English in the section entitled "further reading" and left the German sources in the footnotes.

[17] On page 8 of his *Wagner's Das Rheingold,* Warren Darcy points out the spelling changes in "Der Nibelungen-Mythus," but not in *Siegfried's Tod.*

[18] Darcy, *Wagner's Das Rheingold,* 8.

[19] The study by Curt von Westernhagen, *The Forging of the Ring,* trans. Arnold and Mary Whittall (Cambridge: Cambridge UP, 1976), shows the genesis of the musical language of the *Ring,* but Westernhagen necessarily starts much later than 1848.

The Nibelungs in Germany before 1848

Richard Wagner stepped into a world in which every educated person knew something about "die Nibelungen," but it is difficult to establish exactly what they imagined when they thought about the legend. We can attempt to determine what Wagner himself derived from this legend on the basis of numerous documents ranging from "Der Nibelungen-Mythus," which is contained in this volume, to the entire setting of *Der Ring des Nibelungen,* but it is useful to know the material on the topic that was available to an educated German in the late 1840s, as the notion of a Nibelung opera began to take shape in the composer's mind.

Histories of the Nibelung legend in Germany after the Middle Ages[20] customarily begin with the rediscovery of the *Nibelungenlied* in 1755 by the Swiss physician Jakob Hermann Obereit and its subsequent partial publication by Johann Jakob Bodmer in his *Chriemhilds Rache* (Zurich, 1757), but the Nibelungs had never completely disappeared from German consciousness. The aristocratic world of the *Nibelungenlied* had last been enshrined in the giant Ambraser Heldenbuch — completed in 1516 — a book of medieval texts commissioned by the Emperor Maximilian. Written richly by hand on parchment, the book provided nostalgic views into the feudal past with its choice of medieval narratives and its old-fashioned presentation. Printing had been available for more than a half-century, but apparently no one felt the *Nibelungenlied* would sell enough copies to make printing it worthwhile. Instead printers produced a number of editions of a chaotic adventure tale almost certainly derived from materials totally independent of the *Nibelungenlied* and usually called *Das Lied vom hürnen Seyfried* (The Lay of Horned Siegfried — the title refers to the hardening of the hero's skin to the consistency of horn after bathing in the dragon's blood).[21] This poem tells of a youth raised by dwarf smiths in the forest who doesn't know of his royal heritage until he is told by one of the dwarfs. He sets out to free a maiden from a dragon on a mountaintop, but first has to defeat a giant who is protecting the dragon's lair. He slays the giant and then the dragon, frees the maiden Kriemhild, and takes possession of the treasure. The poem concludes with a brief indication that Siegfried will later be killed by his new inlaws. It is clear that *Das Lied vom hürnen Seyfried,* as it was printed (and reprinted many times) was assembled out of parts from several versions with little attention to how they fit together. One version of the opening has Siegfried misbehaving at home to the point that he is driven out by his parents and the courtiers, while a little later it is

---

[20] Several studies have appeared. The most comprehensive is Otfried Ehrismann's *Das Nibelungenlied in Deutschland: Studien zur Rezeption des Nibelungenlieds von der Mitte des 18. Jahrhunderts bis zum ersten Weltkrieg* (Munich: Fink, 1975).

[21] See the edition by K. C. King (Manchester: Manchester UP, 1958).

assumed that he has never been at home long enough to know who his parents are.

The historical Nuremberg Mastersinger Hans Sachs (whose fictional representation plays a major role in Wagner's *Die Meistersinger von Nürnberg*) adapted this version of the story as "Der Hürnen Seufrid: Tragödie in sieben Acten"[22] (The Horned Seufrid: Tragedy in Seven Acts) and it even spawned a spinoff in the form of the chivalric prose romance *Ritter Löwhardus,* written and printed in the seventeenth century.[23] The *Lied vom hürnen Seyfried* continued in print in various formats through at least 1642. The story contained in the song eventually found its way into a chapbook called *Die Historia vom gehörnten Siegfried* (The Story of Horned Siegfried), which was almost certainly composed sometime in the seventeenth century, although the earliest surviving copy is from 1726.[24] Here the story is even less carefully told than in the poem, and the names are even further from any form known in manuscript or print before. Gunther, for example, has become Gibaldus, and so on. This was the version of the Nibelung legend that was available to many Germans of the sixteenth, seventeenth, and even eighteenth centuries.

In addition, the Scandinavian versions of the story were gradually becoming known in Europe even before the rediscovery of the *Nibelungenlied* in 1755. Following the appearance of the *Edda* by the thirteenth-century Icelandic historian and poet Snorri Sturluson, edited by P. H. Resen and published in Copenhagen in 1665, the *Thidrekssaga* was published in an edition by Johan Peringskjöld in 1715 and the *Völsungasaga* in an edition by Erik Julius Björner in 1737, both in Stockholm and both accompanied by Swedish and Latin translations.

When Bodmer published a portion of the *Nibelungenlied* under the title *Chriemhilds Rache* in 1757, he referred in his introduction to events retold in Torfaeus's *Norwegian History* as demonstrating the widespread knowledge of these stories:

> We read in Torfaeus's *Norwegian History* not only the names Sigurd, Gunnar, Brunhilt, Chriemhilt, but also their deeds, which have a great similarity to the stories told by our poet. There Brunhilt swears an oath that she will marry the one who can break through a burning pile of wood. Since Gunnar was not able to do this, Sigurd took his shape, broke through the flames, and married her under Gunnar's name. He also lay with her, but he did not touch her, because a bare sword lying

---

[22] Hans Sachs, *Der hürnen Seufrid: Tragödie in sieben Acten,* Neudrucke deutscher Literaturwerke 29 (Halle: VEB Niemeyer, 1967). The play was originally published in 1557.

[23] Ernst S. Dick, ed., *Ritter Löwhardus* (Berlin: Weidler, 2003).

[24] The text of the chapbook is included in the *Lied vom hürnen Seyfrid,* ed. Wolfgang Golther (Halle: Niemeyer, 1889), 61–95.

between them prevented him. Because of this there arose a deadly enmity between her and Sigurd's wife, as both went to the Rhine to wash their hair, and Brunhilt wanted to have the higher rank. Sigurd was murdered treacherously on a hunt by his relatives.[25]

Torfæus (actually the Icelander Þormóður Torfason) retold the content of the *Völsungasaga* in Latin in considerable detail without identifying any source more specific than "ancient manuscripts."[26] Bodmer, however, apparently failed to remember several details of the retelling by Torfaeus, who follows the saga closely in having Sigurd killed in his bed, not on a hunt. Bodmer apparently remembered the detail from the *Nibelungenlied* and not from Torfaeus.

Bodmer was seeking an epic poem to set up against the classical epics of Homer, so the chapbook version of Siegfried's deeds would scarcely have entered into his consciousness. He also seems to be unaware of the existence of Norse versions of the story, since he does not know the sources for Torfæus's history, some of which had in the meantime been published. In any case Bodmer made no mention of the chapbook or of the Norse sources, restricting himself to the more prestigious Latin historical source by Torfæus cited above. For this and other reasons, until the turn of the nineteenth century knowledge of these matters was generally restricted to specialists in medieval literature. Otfrid Ehrismann's modern compendium of publications and letters having to do with the reception of the *Nibelungenlied* shows that a small number of enthusiasts were keeping the flame lit by Bodmer alive.[27] The *Nibelungenlied* was finally published in its entirety in Berlin in 1782, but the publication was greeted with deafening silence in most quarters. The edition (along with several other Middle High German poems) was dedicated to Frederick the Great, king of Prussia, who reacted with his famous remark

---

[25] "Wir lesen in des Torfäus Norwegischen Geschichten nicht allein die Nahmen Sigurd, Gunnar, Brunhilt, Chriemhilt, sondern auch Thaten von ihnen, die mit den Geschichten unsers Poeten viel Aehnlichkeit haben. Brunhilt thut daselbst ein Gelübde, Daß sie den heurathen wolle, der durch einen brennenden Holzstoß zu ihr durchbrechen würde. Da Gunnar dieses nicht vermochte, nahm Sigurd seine Person an, brach durch die Flammen, und heurathete sie unter Gunnars Nahmen. Er hielt auch Beylager mit ihr, aber berührte sie nicht, weil ein plosses Schwerdt, das zwischen sie beyde gelegt war, ihn daran hinderte. Zwischen ihr und Sigurds Frau entstuhnd hernach tödtliche Feindschaft, als beyde an den Rheinstrom giengen, ihr Haupthaar darinnen zu waschen, und Brünnhilt den Rang haben wollte. Sigurd ward auf einer Jagd von seinen Verwandten durch Meuchelmord erschlagen." Johann Jakob Bodmer, *Chriemhilden Rache und die Klage* (Zurich: Orell, 1757), viii.

[26] Torfæus (originally Þormóður Torfason), *Historia Rerum Norvegicarum etc.* (Copenhagen: Joachim Schmittgen, 1711), 479.

[27] Otfrid Ehrismann, ed., *Nibelungenlied 1755–1920: Regesten und Kommentare zu Forschung und Rezeption*, Beiträge zur deutschen Philologie 62 (Giessen: W. Schmitz, 1986.)

that the whole of medieval German literature (including the *Nibelungenlied*) wasn't worth a "shot of powder."[28] Although a rallying point for nationalism in later decades, "der alte Fritz" was clearly not at all interested in establishing a German cultural past, especially if the evidence had little or nothing to do with Prussia, his primary concern.

The Nibelung legend did not become a part of popular consciousness, even among educated Germans, until Romantic interest in the Middle Ages combined with German patriotism that was generated in the face of the Napoleonic wars. Lectures delivered by August Wilhelm Schlegel in Berlin beginning in 1803 made the Nibelungs somewhat better known among German patriots,[29] and Schlegel's lectures inspired both Friedrich de la Motte Fouqué, whose play *Sigurd der Schlangentödter* presented the Norse version of the story to the German public, and Friedrich Heinrich von der Hagen, who produced numerous editions of the *Nibelungenlied*, editions and translations of the major Old Norse sources, and commentaries on the Nibelung legend.

Joseph Görres (1776–1848) was in many ways a typical educated polymath of the day.[30] In addition to his interest in older German literature, which led to a number of publications, he was professor of physics in the *Gymnasium* (high school) in Koblenz. In the middle of the first decade of the nineteenth century he became involved with the Heidelberg Romantics, whose views colored his own. Among other things, the Romantic movement saw in popular literature an expression of the *Volksgeist* (popular spirit). This attitude is expressed in his little volume published in 1807 surveying the German *Volksbuch* (chapbook), a term he seems to have invented. The generation of Bodmer had virtually ignored these cheap books, probably never looking upon them as true carriers of the ancient legend. Under the influence of Romanticism, however, Görres sought to present these books as representatives of popular knowledge. He devoted one of the forty-nine chapters of his survey to the chapbook version of the *Historia vom gehörnten Siegfried*. Here he emphasized the role of the North in the development of heroic legend. The *Nibelungenlied* is referred to as a "powerful, wild, heroic work." The chapbook also presents a side of the legend that had been ignored by scholars. Görres gives a very brief résumé of

---

[28] Christoph Heinrich Myller, *Samlung deutscher Gedichte aus dem XII., XIII. und XIV. Jahrhundert*, vol. 1: *Der Nibelungen Liet. Eneidt. Got Amur. Parcival. Der arme Heinrich. Von der Minnen. Dis ist von der Wibe List. Dis ist von dem Pfennige*, edited by Christoph Heinrich Myller (Berlin: Spener, 1784). Friedrich's response is quoted by Winder McConnell, *The Nibelungenlied*, Twayne's World Authors Series 712 (Boston: Twayne, 1984), xii.

[29] *Vorlesungen über schöne Literatur und Kunst*, ed. Jacob Minor (Heilbronn: Henninger, 1884).

[30] See the introduction to Joseph Görres, *Geistesgeschichtliche und literarische Schriften I (1803–1808)*, ed. Günther Müller (Cologne: Gilde-Verlag, 1926).

the story, assuming his readers' knowledge of the legend, and then connects it to the depiction of Siegfried in the "Heldenbuch,"[31] in this case the *Rosengarten,* a narrative in which Siegfried has to fight Dietrich von Bern. His main point here is that Siegfried is seen as a strong and dangerous opponent.

Inspired by von der Hagen's publication of the *Nibelungenlied,* Görres published a long article in 1808 in several numbers of the *Einsiedlerzeitung* in which he recounted many aspects of the Siegfried/Sigurd story as it was known to him from various sources. He mentions both the *Nibelungenlied* (which he knew in von der Hagen's then-recent edition) and the *Hürnen Seyfrid* (with special emphasis on its chapbook version) from the German side, as well as the songs of the *Poetic Edda,* Snorri's *Edda,* and the *Völsungasaga* from the Icelandic. A further source for Görres was the Medieval Latin chronicle of Denmark known, after the appellation of its author, as *Saxo Grammaticus.* Görres mentions all of these things as if they should be well known to his audience, but the Scandinavian works would not be available in German until several years later. Another part of his article concentrates on his perception of the content of the *Thidrekssaga,* a Norwegian retelling of the life of Theoderic the Great based on Low German sources. Since this saga was held to show the ancient roots of the Swedish kingdom in the reign of King Vilkinus, it was usually called the *Vilkina Saga* (although the actual *Vilkina Saga* is only a minor part of the whole work). Much of the article has to do with the concept of myth and the idea that myth arose in the East before the Germanic tribes moved to Scandinavia. Wagner used this notion in his 1849 essay *Die Wibelungen. Die Einsiedlerzeitung* asked for a response from Jacob Grimm, but it ceased publication before Grimm could submit his ideas.[32]

Friedrich de la Motte Fouqué (1777–1843) belonged to the third generation of a family of Prussian military officers that had distinguished itself since the time of Frederick the Great.[33] His lineage went back to the Huguenots who moved to Prussia from France in great numbers in the sixteenth and

---

[31] Scholars of the this period felt that the published "Heldenbuch," which was originally printed in Strasburg in 1483, was a unified work and cited it as such. Confusion is caused by the fact that *Heldenbuch* is used both as a genre identifier and as the title of a specific collection. The original printed *Heldenbuch* has been published in facsimile: Joachim Heinzle, ed., *Heldenbuch.* Litterae 75/1 (Göppingen: Kümmerle, 1981). Görres referred to the specific work, not the genre.

[32] Wagner used the Görres-Gloekle edition of the medieval Lohengrin romance as a basis for his romantic opera, and he derived the misguided "Persian" translation (and spelling) of the name Parzival as "Fal Parsi" or "Pure Fool" from Görres's introduction Joseph Görres, ed., *Lohengrin: Ein altdeutsches Gedicht nach der Abschrift des vatikanischen Manuscriptes von Ferdinand Gloekle* (Heidelberg: Mohr and Zimmer, 1813).

[33] Information on the poet and his life can be found in Max Robert Kämmerer, *Der Held des Nordens, von Friedrich Baron de la Motte Fouqué und seine Stellung in der deutschen Literatur* (Rostock: Adler, 1909).

seventeenth centuries to escape religious persecution. He left his studies in Halle to serve in the military in 1794. After his discharge he set out to establish his reputation as a poet, publishing a number of works under pseudonyms in the early 1800s. Finally in 1808 he published his "reading drama" *Sigurd der Schlangentödter* (Sigurd the Serpent-Slayer)[34] under his own name and was quickly lionized as a major voice in the new poetic movement we know as Romanticism. *Sigurd der Schlangentödter* popularized something like the Icelandic version (largely following the *Völsungasaga*) of the legend among a wider German public.

Richard Wagner never mentioned Fouqué's play, but it is clear that he knew it. In the first place his uncle, Adolf Wagner, had been a regular correspondent with Fouqué during the years leading up to Wagner's birth. Adolf Wagner almost certainly had copies of Fouqué's works in his library. In addition there are many echoes of Fouqué's work in the *Ring*. Elizabeth Magee is only the latest scholar to have concluded that Richard Wagner knew at least *Sigurd der Schlangentödter* as he put together his own image of the Nibelung legend. Fouqué continued the story beyond the deaths of Sigurd and Brynhildis (as he calls them) in two further "heroic dramas": *Die Rache Sigurds* (Sigurd's Revenge) and *Aslauga,* which he published together with *Sigurd der Schlangentödter* as *Der Held des Nordens* (The Hero of the North) in 1810.

Fouqué managed to cover most of the story of Sigurd as contained in the *Völsungasaga* and included elements from the Snorri's *Edda* and even some of the songs from the *Poetic Edda* (even though he maintained that he had had no access to them while writing his drama). Although it is clear that virtually no one in Germany at this time had a real knowledge of the Icelandic language, Fouqué was able, as were many others, to cobble together an understanding of the original through the use of translations, the most important of which were in the *lingua franca* of the educated classes, Latin. The names used in Fouqué's drama are a curious mixture of Norse and Latin forms. Beside recognizable forms such as Sigurd and Gunnar, we have odd spellings such as Grimhildis, Brynhildis, and Gudruna. The genuine Icelandic ending -ur appears sporadically, as in the name of Sigurd's sword Gramur.

Fouqué's drama had the effect of making the story known in Germany in its Icelandic form. Combined with von der Hagen's publication of the *Nibelungenlied* and the ready availability of the chapbook version, it made the story and most of its permutations available to the reading public. Those interested in the Nibelung legend could now inform themselves without having to read the materials in the original Icelandic or in one of the few translations available in 1810, none of which were into German.

---

[34] Originally published in 1808. Reprinted by the author in Friedrich de la Motte Fouqué, *Der Held des Nordens* (Munich: Hitzig, 1810).

Friedrich Heinrich von der Hagen (1780–1856) was born as the illegitimate son of a nobleman in the Prussian hinterland.[35] Early in his life he developed an interest in heroic poems, and collected everything that was available on this topic. He studied law in Halle from 1798 to 1801, where, like many other students, he was a member of a group of like-minded young men who read and discussed literature. Unlike most, however, he reassembled his group after moving to Berlin in 1802 to take a minor legal post and kept it going for some fifty years. Von der Hagen soon became much more interested in early German literature in general and the *Nibelungenlied* in particular than he had ever been in the law. He set out to make the poem available to the educated reader of the time by producing an amalgam that tried to make the original accessible. The result was neither a proper edition — since it changed many spellings and some words — nor a true translation, since it required considerable effort on the part of the reader to understand the archaic meanings and syntax of the language. In 1805 von der Hagen published a number of excerpts from his edition/translation of the *Nibelungenlied,* followed by the full text in 1807. The book also does not seem to have sold many copies. As we shall see, however, its failure did little to dampen von der Hagen's enthusiasm.

Although often subjected to withering criticism by more careful philologists such as Wilhelm and Jacob Grimm, von der Hagen remained in the forefront of the study of Middle High German and Germanic literature. After being granted his doctorate from the University of Jena in 1808 on the basis of his publications and without actually appearing there for examinations, he was appointed to an unpaid professorship in Berlin in 1810 and became with that appointment the first professor of *Germanistik* anywhere. In 1817 he was able to accept a full professorship from the University of Breslau (today Wrocław). In spite of his publications in the field he was unable to garner more than a handful of students for his lectures, and his desire to establish *Germanistik* as a major field of study had to wait for other scholars to join the discipline. He finally achieved his goal — a regular full professorship in the field of German language and literature in Berlin — in 1824.

Von der Hagen was nothing if not active. His publication in 1812 of the heroic songs of the *Poetic Edda* in Old Norse even antedates their publication in the Arnemagnaean edition in Copenhagen (where the manuscript was kept at the time). He published rough translations of these songs in 1814. In the period from 1813 to 1815 he also published translations of the *Völsungasaga* and the *Thidrekssaga* (aka the *Vilkina Saga*). All of these publications took place parallel to his struggle to organize and run the library in Breslau along with his work toward a full professorship at the university. He completed his translations of important texts from the Old Norse thirteen years later with his

---

[35] Most of the information about von der Hagen's life comes from Eckhard Grunewald, *Friedrich Heinrich von der Hagen: 1780–1856* (Berlin: de Gruyter, 1988).

1828 publication of the *Saga of Ragnar Lodbrok* and the *Story of Norna-Gest*. One can question his qualifications as a scholar of Icelandic literature, but the bulk of his translations seem quite accurate. It would have been a miracle if he had managed to translate thousands of pages from Old Norse in such a short time without an occasional misstep. Von der Hagen's translations are particularly important for the present investigation because Wagner acknowledges using them in his work on the *Ring*.

In 1816 another scholar, who later gained great importance in the discipline, Karl Lachmann (1793–1851), entered the Nibelungen fray with the publication of a monograph that set out to demonstrate the "original shape of the poem of *der Nibelunge Nôth*."[36] Lachmann had been trained as a classicist, but eventually established himself in Berlin as a Germanist, gaining a full professorship in 1827. He is held up today as a model for scientific method against both von der Hagen and the Grimms, although few of his main ideas are still current. His teacher, Friedrich August Wolf, had established the dogma that the Homeric epics were put together from shorter "songs," and Lachmann applied this notion to the *Nibelungenlied*. In his 1826 edition of the epic, he claimed that one could recognize some twenty short songs that made it up. The rest, according to Lachmann, was the work of an editor who put everything together using bridge passages that Lachmann did not consider genuine. His edition was the standard for several decades, and Wagner had a copy of it in his Dresden library. Probably more important to Wagner in his formation of a version of the Nibelung legend was a study Lachmann published in 1836 that was also in his library. Most of the book consists of assorted readings from the different manuscripts, but at the conclusion there is an article discussing the Nibelung legend that falls into the same speculative mold established by many of his contemporaries.[37] Lachmann explores the historical roots of the legend and then explores the various aspects of the legend that appear in the German and Norse versions. Among other things, he suggests that Hagen is the murderer of Siegfried, although this notion is missing in all the Norse versions.

Just as important for the early years of *Germanistik* as a field of study as von der Hagen or Lachmann were the brothers Jacob (1785–1863) and Wilhelm (1786–1859) Grimm, who published widely and whose works were a standard source for anyone interested in the Germanic past. Unlike most of the other scholars and poets mentioned above, the Grimms were interested in

---

[36] Karl Lachmann, *Über die ursprüngliche Gestalt des Gedichts von der Nibelungen Noth* (Berlin: Dümmler, 1816).

[37] The article was originally written in 1829 and published in the *Rheinisches Museum für Philologie* that same year. Wagner knew it because it was reprinted verbatim in Karl Lachmann's *Zu den Nibelungen und zur Klage* (Berlin: Reimer, 1836) as "Kritik der Sage," 333–49. My reference is to the latter appearance.

the Germanic past not primarily as a replacement for the classical past (although this also played a role in their thinking) but more for the view it could provide into the thinking and feeling of the *Volk,* the Germanic peoples. They were thus less interested in the aesthetic interpretation of the works involved than in their content, language, and form as evidence of their importance and role in the development of Germanic thought. Their famous collection of fairy tales was intended in this light, that is, as information for a history of German popular thought, not as entertainment for children at bedtime. Each of the brothers was individually responsible for important aspects of Wagner's ideas about the Nibelung legend, so it will be necessary to look at them separately.

In 1829 Wilhelm Grimm published *Die deutsche Heldensage,* an extensive collection of primary materials having to do with Germanic heroic legend over the centuries.[38] Virtually any appearance of a legend or figure of legend in any medieval source, whether literary or historical, is listed here. This collection is still used by scholars attempting to locate references to legendary figures and stories down through the ages. Almost as an afterthought Grimm added a discussion in which he brought together the information he had gathered into a coherent reconstruction of the legends as he found them. This book came out a few weeks after the publication of Lachmann's article on the same subject. Lachmann did not change the article when he republished it in 1836, but added a gracious note suggesting that scholars decide on the validity of the differing reconstruction of the legends.

Perhaps even more important for Wagner's understanding of the Nibelung legend in 1848 was the opus Jacob Grimm published in 1835 called *Deutsche Mythologie* (usually translated as *Teutonic Mythology,* although the title actually means *German Mythology*). Here Jacob made use of his encyclopedic knowledge of even the faintest traces of the survival of German religion in popular superstition along with hints in the surviving literature.[39] He tried not to let himself be led by the much more extensive Icelandic sources, but there could be no avoiding them in the overall structure of his study. This survey was largely responsible for Wagner's ideas about valkyries, gods, and dwarfs.[40] The copy that Wagner had in his Dresden library was of the second edition from 1844.

Of course, the life's work of the Grimm brothers and their overarching notion of collectivism, the idea that the *Volk* — the people — produced the

---

[38] Wilhelm Grimm, *Die deutsche Heldensage* (Göttingen: Dietrich, 1829).

[39] *Deutsche Mythologie,* 2nd ed. (Göttingen: Dietrich, 1844). There is an English translation based on the fourth edition, which was prepared by Elard Hugo Meyer in 1875–78: *Teutonic Mythology,* trans. James Steven Stallybrass (London: Bell, 1882–1888).

[40] Elizabeth Magee addresses this subject in some detail throughout her study *Richard Wagner and the Nibelungs.* There are at least thirty-six references to it in her index, so it is impossible to cite a single passage.

essential ideas of myth and epic as a group, keyed nicely with Wagner's own idea of German nationalism. The composer had derived his notion of a unified Germanic people based largely on his Romanticized view of the ancient Athenians as an ideal society and on his acceptance of the idea that the unity of languages between India and Europe (see below) meant that the Germanic people had come as a group from Asia. The idea that a people could be held together by their attachment to myth was one that led him to choose Germanic legend as a subject for his own dramas in the first place. He idealized the Athenian community and saw in their drama cycles a model for cycles of dramas that would bring together the different parts of Germanic society.[41]

Even more the victim of numerous attacks on his scholarly work than von der Hagen was the Baden historian Franz Joseph Mone (1796–1871).[42] Mone's scholarly career was somehow typical for his age. In 1818, at the young age of twenty-two, he published an edition, with an extensive introduction, of the Middle High German *Ortnit* and offered what he referred to as a "mythological explanation" of German medieval narratives from the thirteenth century. Shortly after this he contributed a volume on Germanic heroic legend to Georg Friedrich Creuzer's encyclopedic overview of mythology.[43]

Throughout his career Mone continued to interpret Germanic heroic legend in terms of mythology, and his efforts found their way into his *Untersuchungen zur Geschichte der teutschen Heldensage* (Investigations into the History of German Heroic Legend),[44] which appeared in 1836 and which Wagner listed as "very important" on his list of sources for the *Ring*.[45] In its opening section we find extensive discussions of the spread of the names Welf and Nibelung and the identity of the names Nibelung and Ghibelline. Following Göttling,[46] Mone related the Imperial party in Italy in the thirteenth and four-

---

[41] Wagner derived his image of the Athenian *polis* from many sources. There are a number of modern studies that explore this aspect: Michael Ewans, *Wagner and Aeschylus* (Cambridge: Cambridge UP, 1982); Jeffrey L. Buller, *Classically Romantic: Classical Form and Meaning in Wagner's Ring* (n.p.: Xlibris, 2001); M. Owen Lee, *Athena Sings: Wagner and the Greeks* (Toronto: U of Toronto P, 2003).

[42] A sketchy biography of Mone is contained in Willy Messmer, *Archivdirektor Franz Josef Mone und seine Zeit* (Östringen: Verlag der Jugendwerkstatt Östringen, 1989).

[43] Franz Joseph Mone, *Geschichte des Heidenthums im nördlichen Europa*, 2 vols. (Leipzig und Darmstadt: Carl Wilhelm Leske, 1822–23).

[44] Franz Joseph Mone, *Untersuchungen zur Geschichte der teutschen Heldensage* (Quedlinburg and Leipzig: Basse, 1836).

[45] In 1856 a Leipziger named Franz Müller wrote to Wagner requesting sources for the latter's Nibelung project. Wagner included a list of sources in his response. The list is quoted in English by Elizabeth Magee in *Richard Wagner and the Nibelungs*.

[46] Karl Wilhelm Göttling, *Nibelungen und Ghibelinen* (Rudolstadt: Hofbuchhandlung, 1816). Göttling's book was in Richard Wagner's Dresden library, but neither it nor its

teenth century, called Ghibellines, to the Nibelungs because of the similarity of their names and because he identified the Nibelung name with Imperial power. Wagner later copied many passages from this portion of the book almost verbatim into his essay *Die Wibelungen* without telling the reader where they had come from. The middle section of Mone's book contains individual discussion of each of the poems of the *Poetic Edda*. These studies are of varying value, but they do not add a great deal to our knowledge of the poems or of the collection as a whole. A considerable part of the book is dedicated to questions surrounding the hoard of the Nibelungs. Finally Mone turns his attention to some outlying sources for German heroic legend, mainly in French narrative verse. Although Mone made important contributions to Wagner's ideas about the Nibelung legend, particularly in regard to the uses to which it was put, his work does not seem to have shaped the composer's ideas about the legend itself, and it is difficult to find any specific parts of either *Siegfried's Tod* or "Der Nibelungen-Mythus" that can be traced back to Mone's work.

Ludwig Ettmüller (1802–77) probably played a much larger role in the further development of the *Ring* poem after 1848 because Wagner made his acquaintance in Zurich and spent many hours in conversation with him about Germanic antiquity.[47] However, Ettmüller's edition and translation of the *Völuspá* (a poem from the *Poetic Edda*, called by Ettmüller *Vaula-Spa*) was already a part of Wagner's Dresden library, so the scholar's name would have been familiar to the composer even before his flight to Zurich.[48] After considerable discussion of published ideas on the metrics and content of the Norse poems, in which Ettmüller does not restrict himself to the *Völuspá*, we find the text of the poem, followed by Ettmüller's translation, which is accompanied by the translator's commentary on the text and a glossary. Ettmüller quotes a stanza from an Old Norse poem that may have inspired the opening scene of *Siegfried's Tod* in which the Norns are shown weaving the rope, which the translator then interprets as meaning "Fate, Death. Weaving this [rope] means to determine these things."[49]

---

author is important to his conception of the Nibelung drama. Göttling's ideas contributed much to Wagner's essay *Die Wibelungen*.

[47] Werner Krahl, *Ernst Moritz Ludwig Ettmüller: 1802–1977: Ein ehemals berühmter Alt-Gersdorfer* (n.p.: Löbauer Druckhaus, 1999). The relationship between Ettmüller and Wagner was the subject of a speech given by Ernst Koch at a 1915 meeting of the Oberlausitzer Gesellschaft der Wissenschaften, "Ludwig Ettmüller und Richard Wagner."

[48] Ludwig Ettmüller, ed., *Vaulu-Spá: Das älteste Denkmal germanisch-nordischer Sprache* (Leipzig: Weidmann, 1830). See also Stanley R. Hauer, "Wagner and the 'Völospá.'" *19th Century Music* 15 (1991): 52–63.

[49] Ettmüller, ed., *Vaulu-Spá*, 54.

Following the discovery in 1786 by the British orientalist Sir William Jones that most European languages were related to Sanskrit, many scholars eventually developed the notion of a common language behind both the Indian and the European branches. Following the now no longer accepted notion that speakers of the same language were related by blood as well, many Germanists adopted the idea that the Germanic tribes had migrated as units from that area and that the legends accompanying them were ancient products stemming from the earliest period.[50] Germanic legends were associated with mythological notions from other peoples. Mone, in particular, liked to associate Germanic legends with those from Greece and the Near East in his syncretistic view of mythology. Wagner latched on to any indication that the myths went back to the earliest times and that they somehow were evidence of the unity of the Germanic peoples.[51] He was particularly drawn to any evidence that the Franks had been the primary Germanic tribe, that their founding legend was the source of Germanic unity, and that it produced respect toward their royal family among all Germanic peoples.

Probably during the summer of 1848 Wagner tried to shape these notions into an essay to which he eventually gave the title *Die Wibelungen: Welt-geschichte aus der Sage* (The Wibelungs: World History Derived from Legend). The essay is dated "Summer 1848" in the *Gesammelte Schriften,* and it may have been begun at that time.[52] But the version that eventually found its way into print was almost certainly the result of later revisions, and the final work was not published until Wagner was safely ensconced as an exile in Zurich in late 1849. It is not translated in this volume, although it is of great importance in tracing Wagner's attitude toward the Nibelung legend, because there is an English translation available in paperback[53] and because this book aims to concentrate on the works that contributed directly to the *Ring* project. The main thing we need to know about this essay is that it traces the Nibelung legend back to the earliest times in Germanic history, before the exodus from

---

[50] An overview of this early development is contained in virtually all histories of philology. I have derived this from W. B. Lockwood, *Indo-European Philology* (London: Hutchinson, 1969).

[51] Wagner's essay *Die Wibelungen* gives ample evidence of this idea. See my discussion of this essay below.

[52] The dating and importance of the essay are thoroughly explored in Petra-Hildegard Wilberg, *Richard Wagners mythische Welt: Versuch wider den Historismus* (Freiburg: Rombach, 1996), see esp. pp. 77–85. Barry Millington accepts her dating in his essay "Der Ring des Nibelungen: Conception and Interpretation," in *The Cambridge Companion to Wagner,* ed. Thomas S. Grey (Cambridge: Cambridge UP, 2008), 76–77.

[53] "World History as Told in Saga," in *Richard Wagner: Stories and Essays,* ed. Charles Osborne (LaSalle, IL: Open Court, 1991), 150–87.

the Caucasus (as Wagner imagined), and sees it shaping history through its embodiment in the Frankish royal family down to Frederick Barbarossa in the twelfth century. The political party associated with Imperial interests at this time was called the Ghibellines, a name that Wagner — following Göttling[54] and others — identified as a version of the name Nibelung via the intermediate stage of "Wibelung." Oddly, Wagner follows Mone and others in placing great emphasis on the treasure, something that he plays down both in *Siegfried's Tod* and in the final version of the *Ring*. In both versions, he causes the ring to symbolize plutocratic power throughout.

Siegfried's Tod and "Der Nibelungen-Mythus," both of which were written in the fall of 1848, show what Wagner made of this wild mixture of sources that were available at the time. "Der Nibelungen-Mythus" shows clearly how he had reordered the various aspects of the myth into a single story that would inform his long-term shaping of the *Ring* cycle. And *Siegfried's Tod* shows how he adapted the legend to the needs of an operatic text. *Götterdämmerung,* which follows the scenes and dramatic situations of *Siegfried's Tod* quite closely, still shows many traces of this theatrical shaping. George Bernard Shaw was not completely wrong when he pointed out that the last act of *Siegfried* and the whole of *Götterdämmerung* were cut from a different cloth than the remainder of the *Ring*.[55] But he was apparently unaware that the aspects he found objectionable (because they didn't fit into his interpretation) were the earliest rather than the latest parts of the *Ring* to be written, and thus not the results of a conversion to monarchism in the composer's later years as Shaw believed. Between Wagner's early versions of the Nibelung legend we find in the two texts translated in this volume and the revisions of the text that led eventually to the four-part festival play we know, there was a considerable period of time and an even greater upheaval of Wagner's situation, as he moved from being an employee of the kingdom of Saxony to being a fugitive in Switzerland. We should probably be amazed that the events of the scenario and of the operatic text survived as much as they did in the final version.

The Versification of the New Text

The text of *Lohengrin* was generally in couplets with end rhyme, the form in which virtually all opera texts in German in this period were written. Wagner had used it for all of his libretti up to 1848, apparently without considering alternatives. The switch, in *Siegfried's Tod,* to alliterative verse with a new

---

[54] Karl Wilhelm Göttling, *Nibelungen und Gibelinen* (Rudolstadt: Hof-, Buch- und Kunsthandlung, 1816).

[55] George Bernard Shaw, *The Perfect Wagnerite: A Commentary on the Ring of the Niblungs* (Chicago and New York: Herbert S. Stone, 1899).

rhythmic organization was a momentous choice on Wagner's part, but it is something about which we have little information prior to the text itself. The usual source for Wagner's thought on the matter was written *post facto* in 1850 as part of his book-length theoretical essay *Oper und Drama*.[56] The discussion there has the character of a justification after the fact, as do many of Wagner's writings. It may be helpful to point to a few sources for information about the verse form.

During the Middle Ages, German poetry moved even more decidedly to end rhyme than English poetry had done.[57] There is nothing in German comparable to the "alliterative revival" in the fourteenth and fifteenth centuries in England. Several poets, most importantly Friedrich Klopstock, had written poetry in lines of free length without end rhyme, but this was not inspired by medieval Germanic models. Even the medieval poetry imitated by some of the Romantics used end rhyme.

The system of alliteration used in Germanic verse was not simply the use of repeated initial consonants as a decoration as in much verse both with and without end rhyme. Shakespeare's line from *Twelfth Night* "Methought she purged the air of pestilence" (I, 1) uses alliteration (on *p*), but it is not structured around it. Ancient Germanic verse from Old English to Old Icelandic builds its verse around the idea of two half-lines bound by two or three words that bear both stress and alliteration. The initial line of the first full stanza of the first lay of Sigurd in the *Poetic Edda* shows this clearly: "Mér hefir Sigurðr selda eiða" (To me has Sigurd sworn oaths). The repetition of "s" in both half lines binds them together. The first stressed word in the second half line is the main carrier of the alliteration. We can almost always recognize the way the lines are bound together if we identify the initial sound of this first stressed word. The rules governing the distribution of stressed and unstressed syllables are very complicated and are still today the object of intense study. It is thus no wonder that the first attempts to describe this verse form in the early nineteenth century were less than perfect. Wagner derived his notion of alliterative verse from these descriptions combined with his own sense of poetry to be set to music.

The use of alliterative Germanic verse as a model in the nineteenth century only began when Icelandic poetry from the thirteenth century became known in Germany. The early translators of Scandinavian materials on the Nibelung

---

[56]The book was begun in 1850 and finally reached print in 1852. Richard Wagner, *Oper und Drama* (Leipzig: Weber, 1852).

[57] It is possible that end rhyme in German is older than in English. Cf. Edward R. Haymes, "From Alliteration to Rhyme: Facts and Conjectures Concerning the Gap in Transmission of German Traditional Verse," in *"Er ist ein wol gevriunder man"*: *Essays in Honor of Ernst S. Dick on the Occasion of His Eightieth Birthday,* ed. Karen McConnell and Winder McConnell (Hildesheim: Olms, 2009), 177–90.

legend in the early part of the nineteenth century did not automatically imitate the alliterative verse of the originals. Fouqué made sporadic use of alliteration in his Nibelung verse-drama *Sigurd der Schlangentödter,* but he did not follow the Germanic pattern with any consistency. Von der Hagen had published an Old Norse version of the *Poetic Edda* in 1812 and a rough translation in 1814, but he made no attempt to reproduce the verse form or the alliteration. The listing by Curt von Westernhagen of the books in Wagner's Dresden library includes von der Hagen's original publication in Old Icelandic, but not the translation.

Wagner's library did include, as already mentioned, the translation of the *Völuspá* by Ludwig Ettmüller, which includes a brief description of the nature of Germanic alliteration.[58] Wagner took out Ettmüller's later book of translations of other *Edda* songs about the Nibelungs from the Royal Library in Dresden on October 21, 1848,[59] a volume that contains far more complete discussions of the rules for alliterative verse than Ettmüller's earlier translation of the *Völuspá*. There is no way to determine whether this book influenced the verse form of the libretto of *Siegfried's Tod,* which Wagner was in the process of writing at the time. Certainly the book and later its author had an influence on the shape of the remaining operas of the *Ring,* since Wagner met and learned a great deal from Ettmüller in Zurich, as has already been remarked. In addition to the influence of scholars like Ettmüller, Wagner's choice of a new verse form was undoubtedly influenced by his choice of Germanic legend, which had been composed in alliterative verse, as his subject for the new opera.

Wagner was probably experiencing frustration with the established end-rhyme scheme he had used up to that point, and the reasons he put forth later cannot be dismissed out of hand. He spends many pages on the advantages of alliteration over end rhyme in *Oper und Drama.* Interestingly, he does not use a great deal of that space to point to medieval German, Icelandic, and Old English poetry, all of which were built on alliteration. His main emphasis here is on alliteration as a way of calling attention to the most important words in a verse. He does make a somewhat stronger bow to Germanic antiquity in his

---

[58] An extensive survey of the translations of the *Edda* into German was carried out by Wolfgang Golther in "Die Edda in deutscher Nachbildung," available in *Zur deutschen Sage und Dichtung: Gesammelte Aufsätze* (Berlin and Leipzig: Behr, 1914), 215–41, though originally published in the *Zeitschrift für vergleichende Literaturgeschichte* in 1893. Golther does not, however, mention Ettmüller's translation of the *Völuspá,* which found its way into Wagner's library. An exploration of the influence of the Old Norse poem on the *Ring* is found in the article by Stanley R. Hauer, "Wagner and the 'Völospá'[*sic*]," *19th Century Music* 15 (1991): 52–63.

[59] Magee, *Richard Wagner and the Nibelungs,* 214.

Mitteilung an meine Freunde,[60] written shortly after *Oper und Drama.* After his description of end rhyme as it had been used, he remarks that "I would have had to abandon my 'Siegfried' if I had had to compose it in this verse [form]."[61] He concludes: "It was this alliterative verse that fitted itself to the most natural and lively rhythm according to the true accents of speech and made possible an infinite variety of expression in which the people themselves made poetry, when they were still poets and mythmakers."[62]

Wagner's use of alliteration and of the verse forms associated in his mind with Germanic verse changed somewhat between the time he drafted *Siegfried's Tod* and the expansion and revision of the entire poem that became *Der Ring des Nibelungen.* Probably the most thorough examination of Wagner's use of alliteration and the verse forms he derived from it is found in the dissertation by Hermann Wiessner originally published in 1924.[63] Wiessner expends considerable energy to show that Wagner's use of alliteration derives almost entirely from Ettmüller's description in his translation of the Nibelung poems of the *Edda.*[64]

Almost more important than alliteration was the new verse form Wagner developed. Although it may have been inspired by Germanic verse forms, at least those from Iceland described by Ettmüller, it was — in 1848 in any case — unique to Wagner. If one reads his description of the new verse required of true drama, there is almost as much emphasis on the rhythmic organization and its approximation of true speech as on the alliteration itself. Robert Bailey has pointed out that the earlier verse, consisting as it had of couplets built around iambs and trochees, had constricted the composer to a four-beat pattern.[65] He found only tiny passages of triple time in *Tannhäuser* and *Lohengrin,* but already in the musical sketches for *Siegfried's Tod,* the first time sig-

---

[60] Richard Wagner, *Eine Mitteilung an meine Freunde* contained in Richard Wagner, *Sämtliche Schriften und Dichtungen,* 4, 230–345.

[61] "Den 'Siegfried' mußte ich geradesweges fahren lassen, wenn ich ihn nur in diesem Verse hätte ausführen können." Wagner, *Sämtliche Schriften und Dichtungen,* 4:570.

[62] "Es war dieß der, nach dem wirklichen Sprachaccente zur natürlichsten und lebendigsten Rhythmik sich fügende, zur unendlich mannigfaltigsten Kundgebung jederzeit leicht sich befähigende, stabgereimte Vers, in welchem einst das Volk selbst dichtete, als es eben noch Dichter und Mythenschöpfer war." Wagner, *Sämtliche Schriften und Dichtungen,* 4:570.

[63] Hermann Wiessner, *Der Stabreimvers in Richard Wagners "Ring des Nibelungen"* (Berlin: Matthiesen, 1924), reprinted in 1967 by Kraus Reprint.

[64] Ludwig Ettmüller, *Die Lieder der Edda von den Nibelungen: Stabreimende Verdeutschung nebst Erläuterungen* (Zurich: Orell, Füßli, 1837).

[65] Robert Bailey, "Wagner's Musical Sketches for *Siegfrieds Tod,*" in *Studies in Music History: Essays for Oliver Strunk,* ed. Harold Powers (Princeton: Princeton UP, 1968), 459–94.

nature calls for a 6/4 measure to accompany the Norns. Wagner later re-marked that the new style of verse-making had made composition almost easy:

> I am now beginning the music, with which I really propose to enjoy myself. That which you cannot even imagine is happening quite of its own accord. I tell you, the musical phrases make themselves for these stanzas and periods, without my even having to take pains with them; it all grows out of the ground as if it were wild.[66]

Wagner's Nibelung Texts of 1848 and the *Nibelungenlied*

The *Nibelungenlied* is one of the most important works of the German Middle Ages.[67] It has drawn scholarly interest almost since it was rediscovered in 1755, and as the huge bibliography on the work shows, it remains endlessly fascinating both to scholars and to lay interpreters.[68] In spite of its importance as a work of art, one can see how some readers have had their difficulties with it. The Middle High German epic is grounded in a fictional world that reflects the politics and social concerns of its own times, the beginning of the thirteenth century. The opening *aventiure* (as the chapters in the manuscripts and editions of the *Nibelungenlied* are called) for example, is a relatively pedestrian description of the main court offices and their holders among the Burgundians in Worms on the Rhine. It concludes with a dream that afflicts the young princess Kriemhild and is interpreted as the prophecy of her eventual marriage to a doomed hero. The heathen gods are, naturally, banned from the Christian world of the poem. Writing about the Huns, who are heathen and who play a considerable role in the second part of the epic, the poet remarks only that they sing the mass very differently (strophe 1851).[69] One can understand how the work might disappoint anyone searching for the gods and heroes, dwarfs and giants of the ancient Germanic peoples. The history of the reception of the poem recounted above is at once the story of an attempt to fit the work into a mold it was never intended to fill, that of the German national epic, and the gradual addition of details from the Icelandic versions of the story in the

---

[66] Quoted by Bailey, "Wagner's Musical Sketches for *Siegfrieds Tod*," 479.

[67] A longer version of this section appears in the journal *Studies in Medievalism* 17 (2009): 218–46.

[68] See for example: Edward R. Haymes, *The Nibelungenlied: History and Interpretation* (Urbana and Chicago: U of Illinois P, 1986).

[69] All quotations from the *Nibelungenlied* are from *Das Nibelungenlied: Nach der Ausgabe von Karl Bartsch herausgegeben von Helmut de Boor,* 22nd ed. (Wiesbaden: Brockhaus, 1988). All translations are my own and are designed to be literal rather than poetic.

numerous attempts to get at a Nibelung legend behind both the *Nibelungenlied* and its Icelandic cousins. At the same time philologists were working toward a far more "scientific" approach to the work leading to the editions and interpretations of the work that have involved scholars down to the present day.

Richard Wagner was one who was disappointed in the *Nibelungenlied*. Since Wagner played down the importance of the work in the formation of his version of the Nibelung legend, most scholars have followed his lead and minimized its role in his creative process as well. Even Elizabeth Magee, who has presented us with the most exhaustive study of Wagner's use of his sources, *Richard Wagner and the Nibelungs,* pays the epic little heed.[70] Much of Wagner's notion of a Nibelungen myth was derived from Scandinavian, or more specifically Icelandic sources. Suffice it to say that the notion of the cursed ring is present both in the *Poetic Edda* and the *Völsungasaga*. The building of the fortress is derived from Snorri's *Edda*. Wagner derived other notions for his *Ring* from various sources, such as Jacob Grimm's massive *Deutsche Mythologie* or the collection of *Kinder- und Hausmärchen* by both brothers Grimm, but we cannot really ignore the influence of the "teutsche Ilias," as some scholars of the early nineteenth century called the *Nibelungenlied,* both on the libretto for *Siegfried's Tod* and on Wagner's concept of the Nibelung legend as presented in his "Nibelungen-Mythus." Wagner chose to ignore the fact that the *Nibelungenlied* is quite incompatible with the Icelandic poetry and prose sources he preferred, and saw all of these works as evidence of a single Nibelung myth.

Those who choose to excoriate Wagner for his failure to represent the medieval versions accurately ignore the fact that the medieval authors, particularly the anonymous poet of the *Nibelungenlied,* did exactly the same, taking an existing legend and re-expressing it in the language and social structure of their own times.[71] The *Nibelungenlied* assumes the social structure of the year 1200, not the year 436 (the historical time when the Burgundian kings met their deaths), as the basis for its highly political version of the story. Siegfried and Kriemhild engage in a courtly love relationship that was so modern at the time that it would have had no meaning even fifty years earlier. The problematic question of vassalage and its influence on the Hagen figure was somewhat older (probably beginning early in the twelfth century), but it too is a product of its times. Wagner made similar use of ancient stories to explore political, philosophical, and psychological matters appropriate to the middle of the nineteenth century. In this respect Wagner was more like the poet of the *Nibelungenlied* than he would have been willing to admit. He was a poet

[70] Elizabeth Magee, *Richard Wagner and the Nibelungs.*

[71] Cf. for example R. G. Finch, "The Icelandic and German Sources of Wagner's *Ring of the Nibelung,*" *Leeds Studies in English* 17 (1986): 1–23.

working from traditional materials in an attempt to express the concerns of his own time.

We don't know when Wagner first read the *Nibelungenlied,* but his Dresden library included three editions of the epic as well as a translation by Karl Simrock into the German of his time.[72] He apparently tried to read the Middle High German text as well as the translation by Simrock. In his famous 1856 letter to Franz Müller in Weimar he mentions the edition by Karl Lachmann as well as Lachmann's studies on the epic (cited above), but does not mention the translations.[73]

The names used in *Siegfried's Tod* and in the "Nibelungen-Mythus" are generally the German forms, even in those places where the Icelandic texts govern the events. Some of these German forms are derived from the *Nibelungenlied* itself, although most of them reflect what were thought in the nineteenth century to be the "real" names. For example "Siegfried" is the form of the protagonist's name universally adopted in Germany, although we occasionally run into forms such as "Sigfrid." The Middle High German text of the *Nibelungenlied* uses the contracted form "Sîfrid," but the circumflex accent in the first syllable indicates a contraction, and the usual assumption is that the first syllable was originally "Sigi." The variant spellings do not affect the meaning of the syllable: "Sieg" or "Sigi" means "victory" no matter where it occurs or how it is spelled. The name "Siegmund" has been changed to fit with Wagner's spelling of his son's name. The most common forms in the Germany of the nineteenth century were "Sigmund" (as in Freud) and "Sigismund." Wagner followed the *Nibelungenlied* in calling Siegfried's mother "Sieglinde," using the same spelling of the opening syllable he had used in the father's name. The names in the *Nibelungenlied* are "Sigemunt" and "Sigelint," but, of course, they are not twins as their Icelandic models had been.

The spelling "Wotan" is Wagner's invention. The most common spelling for the German god, one Wagner had used both in *Lohengrin* and in his sketches for the *Ring,* was "Wodan." Jacob Grimm had listed all the different spellings he was aware of,[74] but Wagner's spelling was new, being a combination of "Wodan," the north German form, and "Wuotan," from the south. The Norse version is "Óðinn." "Brünnhilde" is Wagner's own spelling, built

---

[72] Curt von Westernhagen, *Richard Wagners Dresdener Bibliothek 1842 bis 1849* (Wiesbaden: Brockhaus, 1966), 99.

[73] The most important edition in Middle High German was *Der Nibelunge Not mit der Klage,* ed. Lachmann (Berlin, 1826). The translation by Karl Simrock is *Das Nibelungenlied,* 3rd printing (Stuttgart and Tübingen: Cotta, 1843). The letter to Müller is quoted in English translation by Magee, *Richard Wagner and the Nibelungs,* 18–19.

[74] Jacob Grimm, *Deutsche Mythologie,* 2nd edition of reprint (Wiesbaden: Drei Lilien Verlag, 1992, originally 1835, repr. of 4th edition 1877), 3:48–61. Wagner owned the second edition of 1844.

on the medieval form of the name found in the *Nibelungenlied*, "Prünhilt." (The initial "p" here is the result of the tendency of south German dialects to unvoice consonants.) The Old Norse version of the name was Brynhild, or Brynhildr,[75] and the (Latinized) Gothic form found in the writings of Gregory of Tours, the fifth-century Frankish historian, is "Brunichildis." It is possible that Wagner spelled the name in this fashion to emphasize its roots in "Brünne" (English "byrnie," i.e. upper-body chain mail) and "Hild" ("battle").

Wagner chose the Norse "Guðrún" in a German form "Gutrune" for the final text of the *Ring*, although he used a transitional form, "Gudrune," in *Siegfried's Tod*. He probably adopted the final spelling in order to facilitate Siegfried's pun on "gute Runen" (good runes) that appears in *Siegfried's Tod*. Siegfried's queen in the *Nibelungenlied* is "Kriemhild" (spelled "Chriemhilt" in most manuscripts) a form that is related to the Norse "Grimhild" or "Grim-hildr." Wagner follows the *Völsungasaga* in assigning this name to the mother of Gunther and Hagen. Gunther's name remains unchanged from the Middle High German, although the name appears as Gunnar in Old Norse. The *Nibelungenlied* usually uses the three-syllable form of the name "Hagene," but by the nineteenth century the name had established itself as "Hagen." The Norse version is Högni. The character Gibiche, the father of Gunther and his siblings, although he is called by that name in several later texts and in one manuscript of the *Nibelungenlied*, appears in the thirteenth-century epic as Dancrat. We have no way of knowing how the latter name entered the legend. Wagner simplifies the name to Gibich. The name Alberich is derived from the *Nibelungenlied* as well, although its bearer is a very different kind of dwarf than the Icelandic Andvari, who had cursed the ring when the god Loki took it from him.

In order to emphasize the importance of Siegfried's role in the Nibelung myth Wagner chose to employ the Norns, the Three Fates of Norse mythol-ogy. In *Siegfried's Tod* the Norns tell of pivotal events in the past: Alberich's theft of the gold and his making a ring from it; the gods' payment for the fortress with the ring; Siegfried's killing of the dragon and his awakening of Brünnhilde; and finally Wotan's exchange of an eye for wisdom at the Norns' spring. Wagner extends each of these episodes (except for the last) into the future with a brief text that prepares for the tragic drama about to unfold. During this opening scene of *Siegfried's Tod* the Norns protect the rope of Fate, which "binds the world."

The second scene, in which Brünnhilde sends Siegfried forth to new deeds, was inserted into the text of *Siegfried's Tod* already prior to the copy we have, that is, probably in November of 1848, in response to advice from

---

[75] The final "r" is the Icelandic nominative ending. Most translators leave it off, since it really is an inflectional ending.

Eduard Devrient that Wagner show Siegfried and Brünnhilde as a happy couple before things begin to unravel.[76] In the course of this farewell scene, Siegfried gives the ring to Brünnhilde. Following an orchestral passage depicting Siegfried's descent to the Rhine, we find ourselves in the hall of the Gibichungs, with Gibich's offspring Gunther and Gutrune and their half-brother Hagen in a scene adapted largely from Siegfried's arrival in Worms in the *Nibelungenlied*. Wagner derived the idea of Hagen as a half-brother, whose father was a supernatural being, from the *Þiðrekssaga*, but he then simplified this notion and made it more telling by making him the son of the evil genius of the Nibelung legend in his version, Alberich.

Hagen's role as Siegfried's main adversary is prefigured in the *Nibelungenlied*, a role he does not play in the Icelandic versions. In fact he argues against killing Sigurd in both the "Brot af Sigurðarkviða" (Fragment of a Sigurd Lay) — a poem from the *Poetic Edda* — and in the *Völsungasaga*. In the *Nibelungenlied* Hagen is already mentioned by a concerned Sigemunt as an obstacle to Siegfried's expressed plan to woo the Burgundian princess Kriemhild:

> If there were no one else   than Hagen the warrior,
> who can arrogantly   show his prowess,
> So that I greatly fear   that it would bring us harm
> If we were to woo   that most noble maiden. (54)

> [Ob ez ander niemen wære   wan Hagene der degen
> der kan mit übermüete   der hôhverte pflegen,
> daz ich des sêre fürhte   ez müg' uns werden leit,
> ob wir werben wellen   die vil hêrlîchen meit.]

In spite of parental warnings, Siegfried decides to set out on his own, accompanied in the *Nibelungenlied* by eleven other knights, to win Kriemhild.

Although he is not an immediate member of the royal family as he is in the Norse versions of the story and in *Siegfried's Tod*, Hagen's position as main counselor to Gunther is also established in the *Nibelungenlied*. When Siegfried arrives in Worms, it is Hagen who, like his counterpart in Wagner's works, prepares Gunther and his court with a carefully tailored version of Siegfried's past. In Hagen's narration, Siegfried is reported to have killed a dragon and bathed in its blood, becoming invulnerable. He is also reported to have gained great riches from the brothers Schilbung and Nibelung, whose inherited treasure he agreed to help them divide, but, having been unable to reach an equitable division, he simply killed them and took the treasure for himself. The

---

[76] Wagner refers to this expansion in his autobiography, *Mein Leben,* ed. Martin Gregor-Dellin (Mainz and Munich: Schott-Piper, 1983), 394. The Norn scene discussed in the previous paragraph was also added at this time.

"fee" the brothers had offered Siegfried was the sword Balmung.[77] After killing the brothers, Siegfried leaves the dwarf Alberich in charge of the defense of
the land of the Nibelungs and the treasure. The *Nibelungenlied* is the only
medieval text that separates the killing of the dragon from the winning of the
treasure.

Wagner adapts the arrival scene in the *Nibelungenlied* by having Hagen
introduce Siegfried and give information about his past even before he has
been sighted. There is no source for this in the Norse poems or prose. Like the
Hagen of the epic, the operatic Hagen provides only the information he
wishes his hearers to have, leaving out the crucial fact of Siegfried's relationship to Brünnhilde. Wagner's *Tarnhelm,* or magic helmet, is derived from
what is probably a misreading of the language of the *Nibelungenlied.* Among
the treasures Siegfried wins from the Nibelung brothers is a "tarnkappe" or a
"tarnhût." Many nineteenth-century readers of the poem read both of these
terms as referring to some kind of headgear. The "kappe" of the first word,
however, shares an etymological ancestor with English "cape" and the "hût"
of the second word actually denotes the pelt of an animal, related to the
English "hide." The garment was a cape or cloak that made its wearer invisible, a more or less logical notion within the limited magic of the *Nibelungenlied.* Wagner made a further change by making it into a helmet, usually
represented by a piece of chain mail on stage.[78] In order to reach this form he
may have combined the *tarnkappe* with the "helmet of terror," the "ægishjálmr" of the *Völsungasaga,* but there is no indication that this device is
supposed to make anyone invisible: it only serves to terrify enemies. In the
Völsungasaga Sigurd finds the *ægishjálmr* among the treasures he won by
killing Fáfnir and Reginn. Wagner also combines the device's ability to make
the wearer invisible from the *Nibelungenlied* with the frequent shape-shifting
episodes in the Norse sources (which are not dependent on any device) to
produce a new mechanism of power that, in combination with the ring, allows
the wearer to change his shape, to disappear, or to travel great distances.

After Hagen's bloodthirsty introduction of the hero in the *Nibelungenlied,* he simply recommends that Gunther and his court give Siegfried a polite
welcome. Siegfried responds to the welcome by challenging Gunther to single
combat, with their respective kingdoms as winner-take-all prize for the victor.
Gunther's brothers are able to mollify Siegfried and convince him to join their

---

[77] Wagner used this name in *Siegfried's Tod,* but later changed it to a name of his own
invention, Nothung, in the final *Ring* poem.

[78] Wagner may also have had help in this misunderstanding from Mone, who suggests a
reading that translates "tarnkappe" as "Kopfbedeckung," head covering. Franz Joseph
Mone, *Untersuchungen zur teutschen Heldensage* (Quedlinburg and Leipzig: Basse,
1836), 162.

court. Ironically, the formulas of politeness used by Gunther to establish peace grant him metaphorically all that he had sought to gain in reality by force:

> The lord of the land spoke: "Everything we have —
> If you can honorably deign to accept it — let it be subject to you
> And let it be divided with you,   persons and property."
> Lord Siegfried then became   a little softer in his mood. (127)

> [Dô sprach der wirt des landes   "allez daz wir hân,
> geruochet irs nâch êren,   daz sî iu undertân,
> unt sî mit iu geteilet   lîp unde guot."
> dô wart der herre Sîvrit   ein lützel sanfter gemuot.]

In *Siegfried's Tod* Wagner reduces Siegfried's challenge and the Burgundians' peacemaking to a single sentence: "nun ficht mit mir — oder sei mein Freund!" (Now fight with me — or be my friend!) The *Nibelungenlied* is the only source for this challenge. In the Norse versions Siegfried's arrival is only important because of the potion of forgetfulness he is given at that point. Siegfried's expressed concern about his inability to offer lands and peoples in return for Gunther's blood-brotherhood may also echo the political implications of the scene in the *Nibelungenlied,* since such concerns are totally lacking in the other sources Wagner used. Wagner concludes the exchange with an echo of the politeness formula cited above:

> Happily greet, o hero,
> The hall of my father:
> Wherever you go
> Whatever you see,
> Consider that your own.
> Yours is my heritage,
> Land and people, —
> Support my oath, Wotan! —
> I give myself as your vassal.

> [Begrüße froh, o Held,
> die Halle meines Vaters;
> wohin du schreitest,
> was du sieh'st,
> das achte nun dein Eigen:
> dein ist mein Erbe,
> Land und Leute —
> hilf, Wotan, meinem Eide! —
> mich selbst geb' ich zum Mann.]

After Siegfried has established himself at court (in the *Nibelungenlied*) by spending a full year there without seeing the object of his quest, matters are

changed when Gunther and his brothers are challenged by Saxon and Danish armies. Siegfried takes over the leadership of the defense and easily defeats the enemies. As a reward he is allowed to see the princess Kriemhild. The courtly ceremony in which they meet is quite operatic in its magnificence, but Wagner wisely chose to omit it. In the epic it has the function of emphasizing the courtly elements of the relationship between Siegfried and Kriemhild. After this episode Gunther hears of a fabulous bride in a faraway land and, at Hagen's urging, asks Siegfried to help to win her. He agrees to do this if Gunther will allow his sister to wed him upon successful completion of the wooing expedition.

Wagner included this bargain in his opera. After tasting the draught of forgetfulness (a motif from the Icelandic versions) Siegfried is filled with passion for Gutrune. He agrees to use his powers to win Brünnhilde, whom he has forgotten, for Gunther. Hagen settles down to watch the hall of the Gibichungs, secure in his knowledge that Siegfried is following his plan. Siegfried uses the Tarnhelm to change into Gunther's shape and forces himself in this shape upon Brünnhilde, since Gunther is unable to win her for himself. After Brünnhilde has been sent off to her chamber to await him, he announces in his own voice that the sword Nothung will guard his honor.

In the *Nibelungenlied* there is no indication that Siegfried has ever met Brünhild before, and the fact that he recognizes her and she him has no more significance than the fact that Hagen recognizes Siegfried upon his arrival in Worms. Many scholars have sought clues to a previous meeting between Siegfried and Brünhild in the text, but there is really nothing there. The Norse sources all include a meeting and even a betrothal between the two, and it was only natural for Wagner and others to assume that this was the "real" shape of the myth. It is important for our understanding of the *Nibelungenlied,* however, to realize that it contains no evidence of Siegfried having previous knowledge of Brünhild, and that we should not read into her words or actions anything that is not there.

Upon their arrival in Iceland/Isenstein,[79] Siegfried claims to be Gunther's vassal. In order to demonstrate this, he takes his place in line behind Gunther as they appear before the princess. This jostling for place in line is reflected in the final scene of the second act in *Siegfried's Tod*. Siegfried then uses the *tarnkappe* to allow Gunther to win the games required to gain the bride: throwing a giant stone, leaping a great distance, and throwing a spear. The opponent in all of these games is the princess Brünhild herself, a woman of great physical strength as long as she retains her virginity. Siegfried aids Gunther by physically carrying him through the games while doing the stone throwing, the leaping, and the spear throwing himself. Fortunately, we are told, the *tarnkappe* provides not only invisibility, but also the strength of

[79] The *Nibelungenlied* uses both names for Prünhilt's realm.

twelve men. Later Siegfried uses the powers of the *tarnkappe* to help Gunther overcome his unwilling bride and take her virginity, making her no stronger than other women. The *Nibelungenlied* is very specific that Siegfried subdues the bride, but does not carry out the sexual act. This he leaves to Gunther. These details become important in the oath scene later in the epic.

Another episode of the *Nibelungenlied* that finds its way into Wagner's text of *Siegfried's Tod* takes place between the winning of Brünhild in Iceland and the marriage in Worms. Gunther and Hagen send Siegfried back to Kriemhild to report their success and to order the court to prepare the reception for the new queen. There is an important scene in which Siegfried plays messenger to Kriemhild and her ladies and in which he demands a messenger's reward, something that would normally only be given to one with the lower status of a messenger. Siegfried plays the role of a person of lower status as a part of his courtly-love game with Kriemhild. In *Siegfried's Tod,* Wagner retains specific reference both to Siegfried's role as messenger — "Heiß' mich willkommen, Gibichskind! /Ein guter Bote bin ich dir" (Welcome me, child of Gibich, I am a good messenger to you) — and to his demand for a messenger's reward — "So sagt dem Boten Dank!" (So say thanks to the messenger). Gutrune does not react to either line, leaving them as strange relics of Wagner's sources.

In the *Nibelungenlied* Siegfried takes along Brünhild's ring and belt as trophies after the bridal night episode and gives them to his wife, Kriemhild. We are not told what he tells her about them. She later uses them in a very public dispute with Brünhild over the relative merits of their husbands. Kriemhild claims that Siegfried took Brünhild's virginity and that, if Brünhild maintains that Siegfried is a vassal, then she, Brünhild, was a vassal's concubine.

The claim that Siegfried had improper relations with Brünhild brings us back to the plot Wagner assembled for his versions of the legend. Here the charge is made by Brünnhilde instead of Kriemhild, and it is much simpler: that Siegfried is her husband, which is true; and that he took sexual advantage of her during the night he spent at her side as Gunther, which is not. As in the *Nibelungenlied,* a ring plays a major role in *Siegfried's Tod.* In both the opera and in its source it is the ring Siegfried took from Brünhild on his night with her in the guise of Gunther. Unlike the author of the *Nibelungenlied,* however, Wagner identified it with the cursed ring of Alberich, a quite different ring in his sources, and thus magnified its importance. In both the *Nibelungenlied* and Wagner's texts the ring is used as evidence of improper relations between Siegfried and Brünhild/Brünnhilde.

In the *Nibelungenlied* Siegfried is called upon to swear an oath to silence Kriemhild's accusation arising out of the "battle of the queens" described above. The men of the court are called upon to form a ring (a detail Wagner retains), and Siegfried raises his hand to swear the oath. We are left in the dark about whether Gunther, who has no interest in having Siegfried's knowledge

spread abroad, considers his readiness to swear sufficient or whether Siegfried actually swears the oath.

Wagner kept the accusation, but placed it in his new context, refashioning the oath into a wonderful piece of theater while still following his source quite closely. We have to admire Wagner's ability to simplify and contract the versions in his sources to what we find in *Siegfried's Tod*. It is also a stroke of genius to simplify all the claims and counter-claims to the single point: had Siegfried taken advantage of his night in Gunther's shape beside Brünnhilde? Both Siegfried and Brünnhilde swear on the weapon that will eventually be used to kill him.

Brünnhilde's betrayal of Siegfried in *Siegfried's Tod* is fashioned after the somewhat contrived betrayal of Siegfried in the *Nibelungenlied*. There it is Kriemhild (i.e. Wagner's Gutrune) who is tricked into becoming complicit in Siegfried's death. Gunther and Hagen claim that the Danes and Saxons have renewed their attack, and as they prepare to go to meet the enemy, Hagen goes to Kriemhild to discover the location of Siegfried's vulnerable spot, claiming that he needs to know where it is in order to protect him there in the heat of battle. Kriemhild tells him of the linden leaf that fell between his shoulder blades when he was bathing in the dragon's blood, leaving a vulnerable spot, and agrees to sew a little cross on his garments there, so Hagen will know exactly where it is. The feigned war is called off and a hunt is planned instead. The poet of the Middle High German epic never explains why Siegfried would wear his war clothing on a hunt, but the "little cross" is clearly visible in the murder scene.

Wagner allows Brünnhilde rather than Kriemhild/Gutrune to carry out this "betrayal," and she gives Hagen the critical information, knowing full well that he plans to use it to kill Siegfried. Wagner has also eliminated the messy bath in dragon's blood that hardened the hero's skin. Instead of that, Brünnhilde tells Hagen that she has magically protected him with spells everywhere but in the back, because she knows that he would never turn his back on an enemy.

The scene in which Hagen and Gunther plan Siegfried's murder is present in some form in most versions of the story, but Brünnhilde's role in *Siegfried's Tod* is most closely related to that in the *Nibelungenlied*, where, although she is not actually present when the decision is reached to kill Siegfried, Hagen had promised to avenge the wrong done to her:

> He asked what was the matter, [when] he found her weeping.
> She told him the story and he promised on the spot
> That it would be paid for by Kriemhilde's husband
> Or for that reason he would never be happy again. (864)

> [Er vrâgte, waz ir wære, weinende er si vant.
> dô sagte si im diu mære er lobt' ir sâ zehant,

> daz ez erarnen müese   der Kriemhilde man
> oder er wolde nimmer   dar umbe vrœlîch gestân.]

Hagen then goes on to force the issue on an unwilling Gunther. As has often been pointed out, the *Nibelungenlied* does not provide a cogent reason for the murder of Siegfried. All of the reasons suggested in the massive interpretive literature to this point rest on interpretations of Hagen's character that are not really made explicit in the epic.

Wagner lets Hagen play the same role in *Siegfried's Tod* but with plenty of motivation derived more from his promise to his father, Alberich, than from a desire to avenge Brünnhilde. Here, as in the *Nibelungenlied*, he is the actual driving force behind the decision to kill Siegfried. As he points out to Gunther:

> No brain can help you; no hand can help you:
> You can only be helped by Siegfried's death.
>
> [Dir hilft kein Hirn. Dir hilft keine Hand.
> Dir hilft nur Siegfrieds Tod.]

In the original text of *Siegfried's Tod*, this would have been the point when the title of the opera was sung on the stage, attracting attention to itself. Brünnhilde provides Hagen with the means to kill Siegfried, and Gunther agrees to the plan after being assured that Gutrune will not be told the truth about the killing.

In the *Nibelungenlied*, Hagen, building on the idea of vengeance for the wrong done Brünhild, further whets Gunther's desire for Siegfried's death by depicting the power that would become his if Siegfried's possessions should come to him:

> except that Hagen
> advised again and again   Gunther the warrior
> [that] if Siegfried no longer lived   there would be subject to him
> many kingdoms.   The hero began to grieve for this. (870)
>
> [niwan daz Hagene
> geriet in allen zîten   Gvnther dem degene,
> ob Sîfrit niht enlebte,   sô wurde im undertân
> vil der künege lande.   der helt des trûren began.]

In Wagner's *Ring*, we find Hagen using the same argument, but tying it directly to the power of the ring itself.

> You will gain great power
> If you win the ring from him,
>
> [Ungeheure Macht wird dir
> Gewinnst du von ihm den Ring,]

The scene with the Rhine daughters at the beginning of the third act of *Siegfried's Tod* stands in a complex relationship to the *Nibelungenlied*. As Elizabeth Magee has pointed out, the Rhine daughters are essentially Wagner's invention, although there were some influences that led to it.[80] One of the clearest predecessors, however, is a scene from the *Nibelungenlied*. Two major differences have led many to discount this scene as an influence on Wagner: first, that the hero in question is Hagen, not Siegfried; and second, the mermaids are in a backwater of the Danube, not of the Rhine. In an episode that has no parallel in Wagner's *Ring*, since most of the figures who would take part are killed off in the *denouement* of *Siegfried's Tod*, Gunther and Hagen are leading the Burgundians east to accept an invitation from Kriemhild's second husband, who is none other than Attila (the Hun), known in Middle High German as Etzel. When the Burgundians arrive at the Danube, the river is swollen and there is no ferry in sight. Hagen sets out to find a ferry to cross the river and encounters two mermaids swimming in a backwater of the river. He takes their clothes to force them to give him information. They first tell him that the Burgundians will ride to Etzel's land. When he returns their clothing, they tell him that the Burgundians will all die there if they enter Etzel's land. They should turn back immediately. Otherwise only the king's chaplain will return to Worms alive. Hagen scoffs at their warning, but they give him further warning about the lords of Bavaria, a land they must traverse, saying that the Bavarians will also attack them. Finally, they tell him how to find and deceive the ferryman, so that he will take them across. Hagen finds the ferryman, kills him, and begins the job of setting his twenty thousand men across the river. On the last trip he throws the king's chaplain overboard. The unfortunate man can't swim, but he is miraculously borne up by the water and washes ashore on the other side, where he can return to Worms alive. Hagen sees this as a confirmation of the mermaids' prophecy, and destroys the boat after this last crossing, knowing he and his army will not be returning.

Wagner retains the dire prophecies of the mermaids, but he has them address them to Siegfried instead of Hagen. Their warning gives him a last chance to avoid losing his life, which he tosses from him with a symbolic clod of dirt. When he wrote *Siegfried's Tod* Wagner had not yet decided on all aspects of the role of the mermaids, nor did he give them names, simply referring to them as three "Wasserfrauen" ("Water-Women") and numbering them like the Norns in the opening scene. At the end of their fruitless encounter with Siegfried, they decide to turn to Brünnhilde in the hope of receiving

---

[80] In *Richard Wagner and the Nibelungs,* Elizabeth Magee cites an illustration by Julius Schnorr von Carolsfeld to a translation of the *Nibelungenlied* that shows three mermaids in the water as Hagen dumps the treasure into the Rhine. She reproduces the illustration as a frontispiece to her book and discusses it on page 66.

the ring after his death. Gutrune twice refers to Brünnhilde's going down to the Rhine, and Brünnhilde refers to the mermaids in her final scene:

> Wise sisters of the water's depths.
> The fire that burns my body
> Will cleanse the ring of its curse:
> You will melt it down and protect it pure
> The radiant gold of the Rhine,
> Which was stolen to great misfortune!

> [weise Schwestern der Wassertiefe!
> Das Feuer, das mich verbrennt,
> rein'ge den Ring vom Fluch:
> ihr löset ihn auf und lauter bewahrt
> das strahlende Gold des Rhein's,
> das zum Unheil euch geraubt!]

In the *Nibelungenlied,* Siegfried is very successful in his hunting, bringing back much game for the hunters' dinner. In addition he catches a live bear and releases it into the midst of the party, causing great uproar until the beast is driven out of the camp. Siegfried then catches up with the bear and kills it, bringing it back to add to the huge stores of meat he has already provided. As the hunters eat their supper, Siegfried asks for wine. It has, he is informed, been sent to the wrong place. Hagen suggests a nearby spring to slake their thirst. Hagen and Siegfried strip off their weapons and engage in a foot race to the spring. Siegfried waits, allowing Gunther to drink first. Then, while Siegfried is drinking, Hagen strikes him with his spear through the cross Kriemhild has sewn onto the back of his garment. Siegfried tries to strike back, but his strength leaves him. He dies, cursing his attackers and finally pleading for the safety of his wife, his father, and his men.

Wagner made judicious use of this material, adopting the hunting camp as a location for the murder in *Siegfried's Tod.* Unlike his medieval model, Wagner's Siegfried spends his time talking to the Rhine daughters and ends up with no game at all. Wagner eliminates the plot device of the missing wine in favor of having Siegfried upbraid Gunther for failing to drink. Hagen also puts in Siegfried's wine an antidote for the potion that had caused him to forget the past. When Siegfried is in the middle of the story that would have cleared his name once and for all, Hagen thrusts his spear into the hero's back. Siegfried tries unsuccessfully to crush Hagen with his shield, echoing a similar attempt in the *Nibelungenlied.* Gunther and his men are surprised, but Hagen insists that he is only avenging perjury. Siegfried, mortally wounded, finishes his tale of the awakening of Brünnhilde and dies.

When Kriemhild, the *Nibelungenlied*'s equivalent of Wagner's Gutrune, is told that a knight's body lies before her chamber, she immediately apprehends that Siegfried has been killed. She remembers her conversation with Hagen, in

which she had told him of Siegfried's vulnerable spot. She correctly surmises, even before she sees the corpse, that "ez hât gerâten Prünnhilt,   daz ez hât Hagene getân" (1010, 4: Prünhilt plotted it   so that Hagen has done it). She runs to Sigemunt, who is in Worms with her, and he laments that he cannot think of revenge in his old age. He also has too small a force there to think of attacking the Burgundians. Gunther and his men decide to hide Hagen's deed and to claim that robbers killed Siegfried. When Kriemhild confronts her brothers, she repeats her accusation of Hagen, but Gunther insists that robbers, and not Hagen, killed Siegfried. Twenty years later, at Etzel's court, Hagen finally admits the deed before Kriemhild, although the narrator lets us know that it is public knowledge that he killed Siegfried, "the strongest of all warriors." In a very dramatic, almost operatic confrontation in which Hagen refuses to rise to acknowledge Kriemhild the queen, she renews her accusation. Hagen responds truculently: "ich binz aber Hagene   der Sîfriden sluoc" (1790,2: It was I, Hagen,   who slew Siegfried).

Wagner's Gutrune is a far weaker personality than her model Kriemhild in the epic. In *Siegfried's Tod,* he builds Gutrune's scene of fearful anticipation from elements suggested by the *Nibelungenlied,* since the Icelandic versions, with their murder in the bedchamber in the wife's presence, had no place for this scene. Wagner replaces this with Gutrune's dull expectation of catastrophe. When Hagen brings Siegfried's corpse onto the stage, he first claims that the hero has been slain by a wild boar, which is an echo of a monitory dream Kriemhild reported to Siegfried before the hunt in the *Nibelungenlied.* In her dream Kriemhild saw how two wild boars had torn her beloved to pieces; this dream is also recalled by Wagner in Gutrune's line "Schlimme Träume störten mir den Schlaf" (Bad dreams disturbed my sleep!). In *Siegfried's Tod* Gutrune turns her rage on all the men until Gunther says that the "wild boar" was actually Hagen. Hagen echoes his model in the epic in his defiant admission of the deed: "Ich, Hagen, schlug ihn zu Tod" (I, Hagen, struck him dead) but we don't have to wait twenty years for him to do so. There is perhaps a final echo of the epic at the moment when Hagen attempts to take the ring from Siegfried's dead hand: the hand rises against Hagen, and all present are shocked and frightened. At this point Brünnhilde arrives and takes charge.

In *Siegfried's Tod* Brünnhilde prepares to join Siegfried on the funeral pyre. The body itself is borne to the pyre by members of the court singing a dirge. At the end, Brünnhilde emerges from the fire with Siegfried, whom she leads by the hand to join the gods in Valhalla.

Of course, Wagner's concerns were quite different from those that moved the poet of the *Nibelungenlied.* The thirteenth-century author set out to explore ethical and political questions of his time, using a traditional story to do it. Except for the mermaid scene and an echo of Hagen's watch over the Burgundians in Etzel's hall, there is little said in either of Wagner's texts of

events after Siegfried's funeral. He also rigorously excludes anything having to do with the courtly world in which the Nibelung drama is played out.

The mature Wagner (like many of his contemporaries) considered myth to be the foundation of a nation, and thus his search for a truly mythical basis for drama has a strongly nationalistic aspect. As already noted, he sought the mythical basis behind a story and considered the actual works of medieval literature to be accidents of history. He referred to Gottfried von Strassburg, the poet of *Tristan,* and Wolfram von Eschenbach, the poet of *Parzival,* as being caught up in an age that was, as he said in a letter to Mathilde Wesendonck, "barbaric and completely confused, an age suspended between ancient Christianity and the newer age of nation-states." Unlike many of his contemporaries Wagner did not idealize the Middle Ages, but instead saw them as a period through which the national myths had passed on their way to what he probably would have considered a more nearly definitive form in his dramas. This is ironic in view of the fact that virtually all of Wagner's materials after *Der fliegende Holländer* (The Flying Dutchman, 1843) are derived in some way from the thirteenth century. Even the sixteenth-century hero of *Die Meistersinger von Nürnberg,* Walther von Stolzing, cites the thirteenth-century poet Walther von der Vogelweide as his teacher. In this we might characterize Wagner as a reluctant medievalist, a medievalist who really did not like the Middle Ages.

Der Nibelungen-Mythus / The Nibelung Myth

Commentary

I N MY TRANSLATION OF Wagner's summary of the Nibelung myth as the basis of a drama I have followed the text contained in Wagner's *Gesammelte Schriften,* which was prepared from the early clean copy dated 8 October 1848. I have attempted to retain the sketch character of the original. Where a term that Wagner used or invented has become accepted in its German form in the Wagner literature — such as *Tarnhelm* — I have retained the German expressions. I have maintained his sometimes questionable interpretations of medieval expressions.

At this point I would like to beg the reader's indulgence. In the introduction to these translations I have tried to bring the reader up to the moment when Wagner first committed the Nibelung myth to paper, followed almost immediately by his first attempt at a Nibelung opera text. This all happened in the fall of 1848. In the following I will discuss how Wagner changed his "myth" in the process of producing the final *Ring*[81] poem he revised and set to music over the next twenty-six years. I will not attempt an interpretation of the *Ring* or even of the "Nibelungen-Mythus" here, but I think it is worthwhile to mark out those points in which Wagner deviated from his own version of the Nibelung myth as he developed his concept from a single opera to a grand cycle.

The scenario was designed only to support the composition of *Siegfried's Tod,* so it treats events before the opera in a more schematic fashion than those that are included in the libretto. The entire first scene of *Das Rheingold* is skipped over and a much more mythological view of the world, probably derived from the Icelandic sources, is presented. The scenario begins in the world of dwarfs (Nibelungs).[82] Wagner also associated the Norse word "Niflheim" with the Nibelungs, although there is only the most tenuous connection through the root "nifl," which is probably related to the German

---

[81] Here, as elsewhere in the book, I refer to the text and translation contained in *Wagner's Ring of the Nibelung: A Companion,* ed. Stewart Spencer and Barry Millington (New York: Thames and Hudson, 1993) as the final text of the *Ring.*

[82] Wagner was the first to make a clear identification of the Nibelungs with dwarfs. Some might say that this identification goes back to the sixteenth-century poem *Das Lied vom hürnen Seyfrid,* in which a dwarf named Nyblung appears, but there is no indication that the dwarfs as a group are called Nibelungs. The term Niflung is used for the people ruled over by Gunnar in the various Icelandic texts and the Burgundians are called Nibelungen in the latter part of the *Nibelungenlied.*

"Nebel," meaning fog or mist. Wagner logically connected the dwarfs, whom he imagines living underground, with the idea of darkness and fog.

Although the Rhine daughters play a role in *Siegfried's Tod*, they are not yet mentioned in connection with Alberich's theft of the gold in the "Nibelungen-Mythus." The mermaids, while representing nature at the very beginning of the *Ring*, also allow Alberich to demonstrate the power of what he considers love — that is, lust — in his laughable attempts to seduce one after another of them. Wagner still retained most of the details of Alberich's power grab in the final text of the *Ring*, although he did a more refined job of combining it with the story of the gods. Probably the most important addition to the story is the promise to give the goddess Freia to the giants as their original reward for building the castle, an idea derived from Snorri's *Edda*. This involves Loge in the story in a new way and allows the introduction of the love motif. It is thus appropriate that Alberich had foresworn love in order to gain the power inherent in the Rhine gold and the ring forged from it. In *Das Rheingold* the Norns are replaced in the final scene by their mother Erda, who allows Wotan to replace his own desire for the power represented by the ring with his desire for the mysterious woman who has warned him.

Most of the next few lines in the scenario provide general background for many points of the *Ring*, points that are often reflected in the dialogue but have little effect on the drama as acted on the stage. The one major change that does end up on the stage is the notion in the "Nibelungen-Mythus" that the giants had put a dragon in charge of the Nibelung gold to protect it against intruders. In the final version of the *Ring*, the giant Fafner actually *becomes* a dragon by means of the Tarnhelm. This change is probably derived from the Icelandic sources, in which the brother of Sigurd's smith Regin, who is named Fáfnir, becomes a dragon as a result of his pure evil. Although there is a great deal of shape-shifting in these sources, there is no mention of a magical medium that allowed Fáfnir to assume this shape there. Wagner already uses the Tarnhelm in *Siegfried's Tod* as a means of changing shape, and it is applied here to provide a rational explanation (in terms of the drama on the stage) for the fact that the giant Fafner is now a dragon.

With the exception of the oddly schematic handling of the Siegmund-Sieglinde relationship, Wagner has made all the changes to the sources necessary for a coherent version of the story between the end of what was to become *Das Rheingold* and the beginning of *Siegfried's Tod*. He only needed to concentrate on the dramatic moments to produce *Die Walküre* and *Siegfried*. There are, however, many small changes in detail that went into adapting the events of the "Nibelungen-Mythus" into *Die Walküre* and *Siegfried*.

In the first place Wagner dispensed with all the generations between Wotan and Siegmund, making Wotan himself into Wälse (a name the god uses as a pseudonym when he appears as the human father of the twins). He made the encounter between Siegmund and Sieglinde even more dramatic, as those

who wait breathlessly for the first act of *Die Walküre* well know. In order to make things simpler and more dramatically effective, he also eliminated Sieg-mund's wife. He did manage to include many of the points touched on in the scenario in Wotan's long monologue in the second act of the same opera. Brünnhilde's disobedience was already connected with the Volsungs here in the scenario, as it is in the final version.

The only major element missing from the story of young Siegfried in the "Nibelungen-Mythus" is the fairy-tale motif of the boy who set out to learn fear. Wagner incorporated this element from one of the Grimm fairy tales into his final version. Wotan grants the winning of Mime's head in the riddling contest to the one "who has never learned to fear," the same formula he used to identify Siegfried as the one who would forge the sword Nothung. Sieg-fried's insistence on avenging his father is also eliminated, along with Mime's informing Siegfried of his father's fate in favor of having Hunding die in the second act of *Die Walküre*. Wagner also felt it necessary to add a confrontation between Siegfried and Wotan as Siegfried ascends to Brünnhilde's rock. Dur-ing this confrontation Siegfried breaks Wotan's spear — the symbol of the god's power.

The remainder of the "Nibelungen-Mythus" outlines Wagner's plans for *Siegfried's Tod* quite closely. The scenario lacks the Norn scene and the open-ing duet between Siegfried and Brünnhilde, both of which were added in the fall of 1848 after the initial scenario had been completed, but before the final version of *Siegfried's Tod* translated in this book.

In *Siegfried's Tod* Wagner inserted a long scene, involving Brünnhilde as soloist and the remainder of the Valkyries singing as a chorus, in which much of the backstory is rehashed. There is no mention of an encounter between Brünnhilde and the Valkyries in the scenario, but much information that is told earlier — such as the punishment of Brünnhilde for defending Siegmund — is communicated to the audience in this scene. Wagner obviously needed a vehicle for getting across the backstory involved. The final part of the scene with its non-sexual rape, on the other hand, is described in considerable detail in the scenario.

The scenario also lacks the scene between Hagen and Alberich that forms the opening scene of act 2 in *Siegfried's Tod*. It is possible that Wagner realized the dramatic power of this scene as he was writing the text and decided at that point to insert it. This encounter between Hagen and his father also com-municates many pieces of information the audience needs to know from the scenario. The remainder of what became act 2 delineates the version drama-tized in *Siegfried's Tod* fairly closely. Wagner made several changes to the version contained in his poetic text of 1848 as it made its way to *Götterdäm-merung*, but those changes will be explored in the commentary following the text and translation of *Siegfried's Tod* below.

The scenario also sketches the final act in great detail, very much as it appears in the final text of the *Ring*. Wagner presents extensive dialogue in the scenario, some of which makes its way virtually unchanged into the libretto of *Siegfried's Tod* and from there into the text of *Götterdämmerung*. The final scene of *Siegfried's Tod*, in which Brünnhilde carries the dead Siegfried to Valhalla, is prefigured in the scenario. Wagner later changed the ending of his *Ring* several more times, so that the conclusion of *Götterdämmerung* bears little similarity to the conclusion of the "Nibelungen-Mythus."

Der Nibelungen-Mythus

(Als Entwurf zu einem Drama)

DEM SCHOOßE DER NACHT UND DES TODES entkeimte ein Geschlecht, welches in Nibelheim (Nebelheim), d.i. in unterirdischen düsteren Klüften und Höhlen wohnt: sie heißen Nibelungen; in unsteter, rastloser Regsamkeit durchwühlen sie (gleich Würmern im todten Körper) die Eingeweide der Erde: sie glühen, läutern und schmieden die harten Metalle. Des klaren edlen Rheingoldes bemächtigte sich Alberich, entführte es den Tiefen der Wässer und schmiedete daraus mit großer listiger Kunst einen Ring, der ihm die oberste Gewalt über sein ganzes Geschlecht, die Nibelungen, verschaffte: so wurde er ihr Herr, zwang sie, für ihn fortan allein zu arbeiten, und sammelte den unermeßlichen Nibelungenhort, dessen wichtigstes Kleinod der Tarnhelm, durch den jede Gestalt angenommen werden konnte, und den zu schmieden Alberich seinen eigenen Bruder, Reigin (Mime-Eugel), gezwungen hatte. So ausgerüstet strebte Alberich nach der Herrschaft über die Welt und alles in ihr Enthaltene.

Das Geschlecht der Riesen, der trotzigen, gewaltigen, urgeschaffenen, wird in seinem wilden Behagen gestört: ihre ungeheure Kraft, ihr schlichter Mutterwitz reicht gegen Alberich's herrschsüchtige Verschlagenheit nicht mehr aus: sie sehen mit Sorge die Nibelungen wunderbare Waffen schmieden, die in den Händen menschlicher Helden einst den Riesen den Untergang bereiten sollen. — Diesen Zwiespalt benutzte das zur Allherrschaft erwachsende Geschlecht der Götter. Wotan verträgt mit den Riesen, den Göttern die Burg zu bauen, von der aus sie sicher die Welt zu ordnen und zu beherrschen vermögen; nach vollendetem Bau fordern die Riesen als Lohn den Nibelungenhort. Der höchsten Klugheit der Götter gelingt es, Alberich zu fangen; er muß ihnen sein Leben mit dem Horte lösen; den einzigen Ring will er behalten: — die Götter, wohl wissend, daß in ihm das Geheimniß der Macht Alberich's beruhe, entreißen ihm auch den Ring: da verflucht er ihn; er soll das Verderben Aller sein, die ihn besitzen. Wotan stellt den Hort den Riesen zu, den Ring will er behalten, damit seine Allherrschaft zu sichern: die Riesen ertrotzen ihn, und Wotan weicht auf den Rath der drei Schicksalsfrauen (Nornen), die ihn vor dem Untergange der Götter selbst warnen.

Nun lassen die Riesen den Hort und den Ring auf der Gnita- (Neid-) Haide von einem ungeheuren Wurme hüten. Durch den Ring bleiben die Nibelungen mit Alberich zugleich in Knechtschaft. Aber die Riesen verstehen

The Nibelung Myth

(As Draft for a Drama)

OUT OF THE WOMB OF THE NIGHT and of death rose a race that lives in Nibelheim (Mist-Home) i.e. in subterranean dark crevasses and caves: they are called Nibelungs; in irregular, restless activity they dig (like worms in a dead body) through the bowels of the earth: they melt, purify, and shape the hard metals. Alberich stole the clear and noble Rhine-gold, carried it away from the depths of the waters and forged from it with great cunning and art a ring that gave him the highest power over his whole race, the Nibelungs: so he became their lord, forced them from that moment to work for him, and collected the immeasurable hoard of the Nibelungs, whose greatest treasure was the tarnhelm, through which one could adopt any shape, and which Alberich had forced his brother Reigin (Mime-Eugel) to forge for him. Equipped with these things, Alberich sought lordship over the world and everything contained therein.

The race of giants, the stubborn, violent ones, created in the earliest times, is disturbed in their natural contentedness: their monstrous strength, their simple common sense does not suffice to counter Alberich's power-mad cunning: they see with concern the Nibelungs forging wonderful weapons that in human hands would later be used to bring the giants to their doom. — The race of the gods, growing to omnipotence, used this division. Wotan enters a contract with the giants to have them build a castle, from which they can safely order and control the world; after finishing its construction the giants demand the hoard of the Nibelungs. The superior intelligence of the gods is successful in capturing Alberich; he must ransom his life with the hoard; but he wishes to retain the unique ring — the gods, knowing full well that the secret of Alberich's power rests in it, tear the ring from him too: he curses it; it should be the ruin of all who possess it. Wotan gives the hoard to the giants; the ring he wants to keep in order to maintain his own supreme dominion; the giants demand it and Wotan gives in following the advice of the Fates (Norns), who warn him of the doom of the gods themselves.

Now the giants cause the ring to be protected on the Gnita- (envy-) heath by a monstrous dragon. By means of the ring the Nibelungs and Alberich remain in subjugation. But the giants do not understand how to

nicht, ihre Macht zu nützen; ihrem plumpen Sinne genügt es, die Nibelungen gebunden zu haben. So liegt der Wurm seit uralten Zeiten in träger Furchtbarkeit über dem Hort: vor dem Glanz des neuen Göttergeschlechtes verbleicht und erstarrt machtlos das Riesengeschlecht, elend und tückisch schmachten die Nibelungen in fruchtloser Regsamkeit fort. Alberich brütet ohne Rast über die Wiedererlangung des Ringes.

In hoher Thätigkeit ordneten nun die Götter die Welt, banden die Elemente durch weise Gesetze, und widmeten sich der sorgsamsten Pflege des Menschengeschlechtes. Ihre Kraft steht über Allem. Doch der Friede, durch den sie zur Herrschaft gelangten, gründet sich nicht auf Versöhnung: er ist durch Gewalt und List vollbracht. Die Absicht ihrer höheren Weltordnung ist sittliches Bewußtsein: das Unrecht, das sie verfolgen, haftet aber an ihnen selber. Aus den Tiefen Nibelheims grollt ihnen das Bewußtsein ihrer Schuld entgegen: denn die Knechtschaft der Nibelungen ist nicht zerbrochen; die Herrschaft ist nur Alberich geraubt, und zwar nicht für einen höheren Zweck, sondern unter dem Bauche des müßigen Wurmes liegt nutzlos die Seele, die Freiheit der Nibelungen begraben: Alberich hat somit in seinen Vorwürfen gegen die Götter Recht. Wotan selbst kann aber das Unrecht nicht tilgen, ohne ein neues Unrecht zu begehen: nur ein, von den Göttern selbst unabhängiger, freier Wille, der alle Schuld auf sich selbst zu laden und zu büßen im Stande ist, kann den Zauber lösen, und in dem Menschen ersehen die Götter die Fähigkeit zu solchem freien Willen. In den Menschen suchen sie also ihre Göttlichkeit überzutragen, um seine Kraft so hoch zu heben, daß er, zum Bewußtsein dieser Kraft gelangend, des göttlichen Schutzes selbst sich entschlägt, um nach eigenem freien Willen zu thun, was sein Sinn ihm eingiebt. Zu dieser hohen Bestimmung, Tilger ihrer eigenen Schuld zu sein, erziehen nun die Götter den Menschen, und ihre Absicht würde erreicht sein, wenn sie in dieser Menschenschöpfung sich selbst vernichteten, nämlich in der Freiheit des menschlichen Bewußtseins ihres unmittelbaren Einflusses sich selbst begeben müßten. Mächtige menschliche Geschlechter, von göttlichem Samen befruchtet, blühen nun bereits: in Streit und Kampf stählen sie ihre Kraft; Wotan's Wunschmädchen schirmen sie als Schildjungfrauen, als Walküren geleiten sie die im Kampf Gefallenen nach Walhalla, wo die Helden in Wotan's Genossenschaft ein herrliches Leben unter Kampfspielen fortsetzen. Immer ist aber der rechte Held noch nicht geboren, in dem die selbstständige Kraft zum vollen Bewußtsein gelangen soll, so daß er fähig sei, aus freiem Willen die Todesbüßung vor den Augen, seine kühnste That sein eigen zu nennen. Im Geschlecht der Wälsungen soll endlich dieser Held geboren werden: eine unfruchtbar gebliebene Ehe dieses Geschlechtes befruchtete Wotan durch einen Apfel Holda's, den er das Ehepaar genießen ließ: ein Zwillingspaar, Siegmund und Sieglinde (Bruder und Schwester) entspringen der Ehe. Siegmund nimmt ein Weib, Sieglinde vermählt sich einem Manne (Hunding); ihre beiden Ehen bleiben aber unfruchtbar: um einen ächten Wälsung zu erzeugen,

use their power; for their simple minds it is enough to have bound the Nibelungs. So lies the dragon since earliest times on the hoard in lazy fearsomeness. In the glory of the new race of gods the giants pale and are paralyzed, powerless; the Nibelungs languish miserably and full of guile in useless activity. Alberich broods without rest over recovering the ring.

In high-minded activity the gods ordered now the world, bound the elements through wise laws, and devoted themselves to the most solicitous care of the race of man. Their power stands above everything. But the peace, through which they have risen to power, is not based on reconciliation, it is brought about through violence and cunning. The object of their higher ordering of the world is a moral consciousness: the injustice they perpetuate, however, adheres to them. Out of the depths of Nibelheim groans the knowledge of their guilt: for the slavery of the Nibelungs has not been broken; the power has only been stolen from Alberich and certainly not for a higher purpose, but rather the soul, the freedom of the Nibelungs, lies buried and useless under the belly of the lazy dragon. Alberich is right at least this far in his accusations of the gods. Wotan cannot erase the injustices without committing a new one: only a free will, independent of the gods, which is willing to take all of the guilt on itself and to suffer for it, can break the spell, and the gods see in human beings the capability for such a will. They try to transfer their divinity to humanity, in order to raise its power to such a level that it, upon becoming aware of this power, turns away from divine protection in order to do whatever occurs to it by its own free will. In order to reach this high goal of erasing their own guilt, the gods now educate human beings, and their goal would be reached if they extinguished themselves in this creation of humanity, namely that they forego their direct influence in favor of the freedom of human consciousness. Mighty human races, bred from divine seed, are already arising: in struggle and battle they are steeling their strength; Wotan's wish-maidens shield them as shield-maidens, as Valkyries they accompany those who have fallen in battle to Valhalla, where the heroes in Wotan's company continue a magnificent life with battle-games. But the real hero has not yet been born, the one in whom the autonomous power would come to full consciousness, so that he — his free will showing him the deadly consequences — would be able to call his boldest deed his own. In the race of Volsungs this hero should finally be born: a childless marriage of this dynasty was brought to fruition by Wotan through the means of one of Holda's apples, which he caused the pair to eat. A pair of twins, Siegmund and Sieglinde (brother and sister) are born to this couple. Siegmund takes a wife; Sieglinde is married to a man (Hunding); but both their marriages remain childless. In order to bring forth a true Volsung, brother and sister come together

begatten sich nun Bruder und Schwester selbst. Hunding, Sieglinde's Gemahl,
erfährt das Verbrechen, verstößt sein Weib und überfällt Siegmund mit Streit.
Brünnhild, die Walküre, schützt Siegmund gegen Wotan's Geheiß, welcher
dem Verbrechen zur Sühne ihm den Untergang beschieden hat; schon zückt
unter Brünnhild's Schild Siegmund zu dem tödtlichen Streiche auf Hunding
das Schwert, welches Wotan ihm einst selbst geschenkt, als der Gott den
Streich mit seinem Speer auffängt, woran das Schwert in zwei Stücken zer-
bricht. Siegmund fällt. Brünnhild wird von Wotan für ihren Ungehorsam ge-
straft: er verstößt sie aus der Schaar der Walküren, und bannt sie auf einen
Felsen, wo sie, die göttliche Jungfrau, dem Manne vermählt werden soll, der
dort sie findet und aus dem Schlafe erweckt, in den Wotan sie versenkt; sie
erfleht sich als Gnade, Wotan möge den Felsen mit Schrecken des Feuers
umgeben, damit sie sicher sei, daß sie nur der kühnste Held gewinnen können
würde. — Die verstoßene Sieglinde gebiert in der Wildniß nach langer
Schwangerschaft Siegfried (der durch Sieg Friede bringen soll): Reigin
(Mime), Alberich's Bruder, ist, als Sieglinde in den Wehen schrie, aus Klüften
zu ihr getreten, und hat ihr geholfen: nach der Geburt stirbt sie, nachdem sie
Reigin ihr Schicksal gemeldet, und den Knaben diesem übergeben hat. Reigin
erzieht Siegfried, lehrt ihn schmieden, meldet ihm den Tod seines Vaters, und
verschafft ihm die beiden Stücken von dessen zerschlagenem Schwerte, aus
welchen Siegfried unter Mime's Anleitung das Schwert (Balmung) schmiedet.
Nun reizt Mime den Jüngling zur Erlegung des Wurmes, wodurch er sich ihm
dankbar erzeigen soll. Siegfried begehrt zuvor den Mord seines Vaters zu
rächen: er zieht aus, überfällt und tödtet Hunding: hiernach erst erfüllt er
Mime's Wunsch, bekämpft und erschlägt den Riesenwurm. Als er seine vom
Blute des Wurmes erhitzten Finger zur Kühlung in den Mund führt, kostet er
unwillkürlich von dem Blute und versteht dadurch plötzlich die Sprache der
Waldvögel, welche um ihn herum singen. Sie preisen Siegfried's ungeheure
That, verweisen ihn auf den Nibelungenhort in des Wurmes Höhle, und warnen ihn vor Mime, der ihn nur verwendet habe, um zu dem Horte zu gelangen, und der nun nach seinem Leben trachte, um den Hort für sich allein
zu behalten. Siegfried erschlägt hierauf Mime, und nimmt von dem Horte den
Ring und die Tarnkappe: er vernimmt die Vögel wieder, welche ihm rathen,
das herrlichste Weib, Brünnhild, zu gewinnen. Siegfried zieht nun aus, erreicht
die Felsenburg Brünnhilde's, dringt durch das umlodernde Feuer, erweckt
Brünnhild; sie erkennt freudig Siegfried, den herrlichsten Helden vom Wäl-
sungenstamme, und ergiebt sich ihm: er vermählt sich ihr durch den Ring
Alberich's, den er an ihren Finger steckt. Als es ihn forttreibt, zu neuen Thaten
auszuziehen, theilt sie ihm ihr geheimes Wissen in hohen Lehren mit, warnt
ihn vor den Gefahren des Truges und der Untreue: sie schwören sich Eide und
Siegfried zieht fort.

Ein zweiter, auch von Göttern entsprossener Heldenstamm ist der der
Gibichungen am Rhein: dort blühen jetzt Gunther und Gudrun, seine

themselves. Hunding, Sieglinde's husband, finds out about the crime, exiles his wife, and attacks Siegmund. Brünnhild, the Valkyrie, protects Siegmund against Wotan's order, who had condemned him to die to atone for his crime. Behind Brünnhild's shield Siegmund is already drawing back his sword for the fatal blow against Hunding, the sword that Wotan himself had once given him, when the god catches the blow with his spear, upon which the sword breaks in two. Siegmund falls. Brünnhild is punished for her disobedience: he exiles her from the Valkyries and bans her to a rock, where she, the divine virgin, is to be married to the man who finds her there and awakens her from the sleep into which Wotan has placed her. She implores Wotan to give her one boon: that he surround the rock with fire, so that she could be certain that only the boldest hero could win her. — The exiled Sieglinde bears Siegfried (who through victory should bring peace) in the wilderness after a long pregnancy. Reigin (Mime), Alberich's brother, came out of the crevasses to Sieglinde when she cried out during birth and gave her aid. After the birth she dies, after telling Reigin about her fate and turning the child over to him. Reigin raises Siegfried, teaches him smithing, tells him about the death of his father, and gives him the two pieces of his broken sword, from which Siegfried under Mime's instruction forges the sword (Balmung). Now Mime incites Siegfried to kill the dragon, through which he should show his gratitude. Siegfried wishes first to avenge the death of his father: he sets out, attacks, and kills Hunding. Only after this does he fulfill Mime's wish: he fights and kills the dragon. His finger is burned by the blood of the dragon, and as he puts it in his mouth to cool it, he involuntarily tastes the blood and understands suddenly the language of the forest birds, which are singing around him. They praise his great deed, direct him to the hoard of the Nibelungs in the dragon's cave, and warn him about Mime, who, they say, had only used him to get to the hoard, and who now intends to kill him in order to keep the hoard for himself alone. Siegfried now kills Mime and takes the ring and the tarnkappe from the treasure: he hears the birds again, who advise him now to win the most magnificent woman, Brünnhild. Siegfried sets out and reaches Brünnhilde's castle on a rock, penetrates the surrounding fire, and awakens Brünnhild. She recognizes Siegfried, the most magnificent hero of the Volsung dynasty, joyfully, and gives herself to him. He marries her with Alberich's ring, which he places on her finger. As he is driven forth to new deeds, she passes on her secret wisdom to him in high teachings, warns him about the dangers of trickery and faithlessness. They swear oaths to one another and Siegfried departs.

A second heroic dynasty, which is also descended from the gods, is that of the Gibichungs on the Rhine. There Gunther and his sister Gudrun

Schwester. Gunther's Mutter, Grimhild, ward einst von Alberich überwältigt, und sie gebar von ihm einen unehelichen Sohn, Hagen. Wie die Wünsche und Hoffnungen der Götter auf Siegfried beruhen, setzt Alberich seine Hoffnung der Wiedergewinnung des Ringes auf den von ihm erzeugten Helden Hagen. Hagen ist bleichfarbig, ernst und düster; frühzeitig sind seine Züge verhärtet; er erscheint älter als er ist. Alberich hat ihm in seiner Kindheit bereits geheimes Wissen und Kenntniß des väterlichen Schicksales beigebracht, und ihn gereizt, nach dem Ringe zu streben: er ist stark und gewaltig; dennoch erschien er Alberich nicht mächtig genug, den Riesenwurm zu tödten. Da Alberich machtlos geworden, konnte er seinem Bruder Mime nicht wehren, als dieser durch Siegfried den Hort zu erlangen suchte: Hagen soll nun aber Siegfried's Verderben herbeiführen, um diesem in seinem Untergange den Ring abzugewinnen. Gegen Gunther und Gudrun ist Hagen verschlossen, — sie fürchten ihn, aber schätzen seine Klugheit und Erfahrung: das Geheimniß einer wunderbaren Herkunft Hagen's, und daß er nicht sein ächter Bruder, ist Gunther bekannt: er schilt ihn einmal einen Albensohn.

Gunther ist von Hagen darüber belehrt, daß Brünnhild das begehrenswertheste Weib sei, und zu dem Verlangen nach ihrem Besitze von ihm angereizt, als Siegfried zu den Gibichungen an den Rhein kommt. Gudrun, durch das Lob, welches Hagen Siegfried spendet, in Liebe zu diesem entbrannt, reicht auf Hagen's Rath Siegfried zum Willkommen einen Trank, durch Hagen's Kunst bereitet und von der Wirksamkeit, daß er Siegfried seiner Erlebnisse mit Brünnhild und seiner Vermählung mit ihr vergessen macht. Siegfried begehrt Gudrun zum Weibe: Gunther sagt sie ihm zu, unter der Bedingung, daß er ihm zu Brünnhild verhelfe. Siegfried geht darauf ein: sie schließen Blutbrüderschaft und schwören sich Eide, von denen Hagen sich ausschließt. — Siegfried und Gunther begeben sich auf die Fahrt und gelangen zu Brünnhild's Felsenburg: Gunther bleibt im Schiffe zurück; Siegfried benutzt zum ersten und einzigen Male seine Macht als Herr der Nibelungen, indem er den Tarnhelm aufsetzt, und durch ihn sich Gunther's Gestalt und Aussehen verschafft; so dringt er durch die Flammen zu Brünnhild. Diese, durch Siegfried bereits des Magdthumes beraubt, hat auch ihre übermenschliche Kraft eingebüßt, alles Wissen hat sie an Siegfried — der es nicht nützt — vergeben —; sie ist ohnmächtig wie ein gewöhnliches Weib, und vermag dem neuen, kühnen Werber nur fruchtlosen Widerstand zu bieten; er entreißt ihr den Ring — durch den sie nun Gunther vermählt sein soll —, und zwingt sie in den Saal, wo er die Nacht neben ihr schläft, zu ihrer Verwunderung jedoch sein Schwert zwischen sie Beide legt. Am Morgen bringt er sie zum Schiffe, wo er seine Stelle zu ihrer Seite unvermerkt von dem wahren Gunther einnehmen läßt, und durch die Kraft des Tarnhelmes sich schnell an den Rhein zur Gibichenburg versetzt. Gunther erreicht mit Brünnhild, welche ihm in düsterem Schweigen folgt, auf dem Rheine die Heimath: Siegfried, an Gudrun's Seite, und Hagen empfangen die Ankommenden. — Brünnhild ist ent-

flourish. Gunther's mother, Grimhild, was once ravished by Alberich, and she bore him an illegitimate son, Hagen. Just as the wishes and hopes of the gods rest on Siegfried, Alberich puts his hope of regaining the ring on Hagen, the hero he fathered. Hagen is pale, serious and dark. His features have turned hard early; he looks older than he is. Alberich has already taught him in childhood secret knowledge and information about his father's fate and incited him to seek the ring. He is strong and powerful; and yet he does not seem powerful enough to Alberich to kill the dragon. Since Alberich had lost his power, he was not able to prevent his brother Mime from attempting to gain the hoard through Siegfried. Hagen is supposed to bring about Siegfried's ruin in order to regain the ring through his death. Hagen is taciturn toward Gunther and Gudrun — they are afraid of him, but they value his wisdom and experience. The secret of Hagen's strange origin, and that he is not his full brother, is known to Gunther. He calls him at one point insultingly an "elf-son."

Gunther has been instructed by Hagen that Brünnhild is the most desirable woman, and is incited by him to desire to possess her when Siegfried arrives at the Gibichungs Hall on the Rhine. Gudrun, inflamed to love for Siegfried by Hagen's praise of him, serves Siegfried a welcoming drink, which has been prepared with Hagen's arts, so that it causes Siegfried to forget his experiences with Brünnhild and his marriage to her. Siegfried desires Gudrun as a wife: Gunther agrees under the condition that Siegfried help him win Brünnhilde. Siegfried agrees. They vow blood-brotherhood and swear oaths from which Hagen abstains. Siegfried and Gunther embark on the journey and arrive at Brünnhild's rock castle. Gunther remains behind in the ship while Siegfried uses for the first and only time his power as lord of the Nibelungs in that he puts on the tarnhelm and through it adopts Gunther's shape and appearance. In this form he penetrates the flames to Brünnhild. She, who has already given up her virginity to Siegfried, has also given up her superhuman strength. All her wisdom has also passed on to Siegfried — who makes no use of it — and she is as weak as an ordinary woman so that she can offer only fruitless resistance to this new bold wooer. He tears the ring from her — through which she is now supposed to be married to Gunther — and forces her into the chamber, where he sleeps next to her through the night, but to her amazement, he places his sword between them. In the morning he brings her to the ship, where he allows the real Gunther to take his place without her noticing. Using the tarnhelm, he returns quickly to the castle of the Gibichungs on the Rhine. Gunther reaches his home with Brünnhild, who follows him in stony silence. Siegfried, at Gudrun's side, and Hagen receive them. Brünnhild is

setzt, da sie Siegfried als Gudrun's Gemahl erblickt: seine kalte, freundliche Gelassenheit ihr gegenüber macht sie staunen; da er sie an Gunther zurückweist, erkennt sie den Ring an seinem Finger: sie ahnt den Betrug, der ihr gespielt, und fordert den Ring, der nicht ihm gehöre, sondern den Gunther von ihr empfangen: er verweigert ihn. Sie fordert Gunther auf, den Ring von Siegfried zu begehren: Gunther ist verwirrt und zögert. Brünnhild: so empfing Siegfried den Ring von ihr? Siegfried, der den Ring erkannt, »von keinem Weib empfing ich ihn; den hat meine Kraft dem Riesenwurm abgewonnen; durch ihn bin ich der Nibelungen Herr, und Keinem trete ich seine Macht ab«. Hagen tritt dazwischen und frägt Brünnhild, ob sie genau den Ring kenne? Sei es ihr Ring, so habe ihn Siegfried durch Trug gewonnen, und er könne nur Gunther, ihrem Gemahle, gehören. Brünnhild schreit laut auf über den Betrug, der ihr gespielt; der fürchterlichste Rachedurst erfüllt sie gegen Siegfried. Sie ruft Gunther zu, daß er von Siegfried betrogen: »nicht dir — diesem Manne bin ich vermählt, er gewann meine Gunst«. — Siegfried schilt sie ehrvergessen: seiner Blutbrüderschaft sei er treu gewesen, — sein Schwert habe er zwischen Brünnhild und sich gelegt: — er fordert sie auf, dieß zu bezeugen. — Absichtlich und nur auf sein Verderben bedacht will sie Siegfried nicht verstehen: er lüge und berufe sich schlecht auf sein Schwert Balmung, das sie ruhig an der Wand hängen gesehen, als er in Liebe bei ihr lag. — Die Männer und Gudrun bestürmen Siegfried, die Anklage von sich abzuweisen, wenn er es vermöge. Siegfried schwört feierliche Eide zur Bekräftigung seiner Aussage. Brünnhild schilt ihn meineidig: so viele Eide, ihr und Gunther, habe er geschworen, die er gebrochen: nun schwöre er auch einen Meineid, um eine Lüge zu bekräftigen. Alles ist in höchster Aufregung. Siegfried ruft Gunther zu, seinem Weibe zu wehren, die schamlos ihre und ihres Gatten Ehre verlästere: er entfernt sich mit Gudrun in den Saal. — Gunther, in tiefster Scham und furchtbarer Verstimmung, hat sich mit verhülltem Gesicht abseits niedergesetzt: an Brünnhild, dem schrecklichsten inneren Sturme preisgegeben, tritt Hagen heran. Er bietet sich ihr zum Rächer ihrer Ehre an: sie verlacht ihn als ohnmächtig, Siegfried zu bewältigen: ein Blick aus seinem strahlenden Auge, das selbst durch jene trügerische Gestalt zu ihr geleuchtet, vermöge Hagen's Muth zu brechen. Hagen: wohl kenne er Siegfried's furchtbare Stärke, drum solle sie ihm sagen, wie er zu bewältigen wäre? Sie, die Siegfried gefeit und durch geheimen Segen ihn gegen Wunden gewaffnet hat, räth nun Hagen, ihn im Rücken zu treffen; denn da sie wußte, daß der Held nie dem Feinde den Rücken bieten würde, habe sie an diesem den Segen gespart. — Gunther muß den Mordplan kennen. Sie rufen ihn auf, seine Ehre zu rächen: Brünnhild bedeckt ihn mit den Vorwürfen der Feigheit und des Betruges; Gunther erkennt seine Schuld, und die Nothwendigkeit, durch Siegfried's Tod seine Schande zu enden. Er erschrickt, sich des Bruches der Blutbrüderschaft schuldig zu machen. Brünnhild höhnt ihn mit bitterem Schmerz: was sei an ihr nicht Alles verbrochen worden? Hagen reizt Gunther

shocked when she sees Siegfried as Gudrun's husband: his cold, friendly attitude toward her astonishes her. When he turns her back to Gunther, she sees the ring on his finger. She begins to suspect the deception that has been carried out on her. She demands the ring, which she maintains doesn't belong to him, but which Gunther had received from her. He refuses. She demands that Gunther retrieve the ring from Siegfried. Gunther is confused and hesitates. Brünnhild: Did Siegfried then receive the ring from her? Siegfried, who recognizes the ring, says, "I received it from no woman. My strength won it from a giant dragon. Through it I am the lord of the Nibelungs and I give up my might to no one." Hagen steps between them and asks Brünnhild whether she knows the ring precisely? If it is her ring, then Siegfried gained it through deception, and it can only belong to Gunther, her husband. Brünnhild cries out loudly against the betrayal that has been carried out against her. She is filled with the most fearsome thirst for vengeance toward Siegfried. She calls out to Gunther that he has been betrayed by Siegfried: "not to you — but to this man I am married: he had his way with me." — Siegfried accuses her of forgetting her honor: he has remained true to his blood-brotherhood — he had placed his sword between himself and Brünnhild. — He demands that she confirm this. On purpose and only determined to ruin him, she pretends not to understand: he is lying and should not swear by his sword Balmung, which she saw quietly hanging on the wall while he lay beside her in love. — The men and Gudrun demand that Siegfried turn away the accusation, if he can. Siegfried swears solemn oaths to support his testimony. Brünnhild accuses him of perjury: he has sworn so many oaths to her and to Gunther, which he has now broken. Now, she says, he commits perjury in order to support another lie. Everyone is in an uproar. Siegfried calls to Gunther to control his woman, who shamelessly insults her and her husband's honor. He departs, entering the hall with Gudrun. — Gunther, deeply shamed and in a foul humor, sits with his face covered, off to the side. Hagen approaches Brünnhild, who is weathering the most intense inner storms. He offers to avenge her dishonor. She ridicules him as a weakling who could never best Siegfried. One glance from his radiant eye, which even in this deceitful condition still shines, would suffice to break Hagen's courage. Hagen says that he knows Siegfried's fearful strength; therefore she should tell him how he can be defeated. She, who protected Siegfried with secret spells against all wounds, now advises Hagen to strike at his back, because, knowing he would never turn his back to an enemy, she spared her spells there. — Gunther has to know the murder plot. They call upon him to avenge his dishonor. Brünnhild covers him with accusations of cowardice and betrayal. Gunther recognizes his guilt and the necessity to end his shame through Siegfried's death. He shrinks from breaking the oath of blood-brotherhood. Brünnhild mocks him with bitter pain. What oaths have not been broken in relation to her? Hagen

durch die Aussicht auf die Erlangung des Ringes der Nibelungen, den Siegfried wohl nur im Tode werde fahren lassen. Gunther willigt ein; Hagen räth
eine Jagd auf morgen, dabei solle Siegfried überfallen, und vielleicht Gudrun
selbst sein Mord verheimlicht werden; um sie war Gunther besorgt: Brünnhilde's Rachelust schärft sich in der Eifersucht auf Gudrun. So wird von den
Dreien Siegfried's Mord beschlossen. — Siegfried erscheint mit Gudrun fest-
lich geschmückt in der Halle, lädt zum Opfer und zur Hochzeitsfeier ein.
Heuchlerisch gehorchen die Verschworenen: Siegfried und Gudrun freuen
sich des anscheinend wiedergekehrten Friedens.

Am folgenden Morgen geräth Siegfried in der Verfolgung eines Wildes in
die Einsamkeit einer Felsenschlucht am Rhein. Drei Meerfrauen tauchen aus
der Fluth auf: sie sind weissagende Töchter der Wassertiefe, der einst von
Alberich das klare Rheingold entrissen, um aus ihm den mächtigen, verhäng-
nißvollen Ring zu schmieden: der Fluch und die Macht dieses Ringes würde
vernichtet sein, wenn er dem Wasser zurückgegeben und somit in das ursprüngliche reine Element wieder aufgelöst würde. Die Frauen trachten nach
dem Ringe und begehren ihn von Siegfried, der ihn verweigert. (Er hat
schuldlos die Schuld der Götter übernommen, ihr Unrecht büßt er an sich
durch seinen Trotz, seine Selbstständigkeit.) Sie verkünden ihm Unheil und
den Fluch, der an dem Ringe haftet: er soll ihn in die Fluth werfen, sonst
müsse er heute noch sterben. Siegfried: »ihr listigen Frauen sollt mich nicht
um meine Macht betrügen: den Fluch und euer Drohen achte ich nicht eines
Haares werth. Wozu mein Muth mich treibt, das ist mir Urgesetz, und was ich
nach meinem Sinne thue, das ist mir so bestimmt: nennt ihr dieß Fluch oder
Segen, ich gehorche ihm und strebe nicht wider meine Kraft.« Die Frauen:
»willst du die Götter übertreffen?« Siegfried: »Zeigtet ihr mir die Möglichkeit,
die Götter zu bewältigen, so müßte ich nach meinem Muthe sie bekämpfen.
Drei weisere Frauen, als ihr seid, kenne ich; die wissen, wo die Götter einst in
banger Sorge streiten werden. Zu der Götter Frommen ist es, wenn sie sorgen,
daß ich dann mit ihnen kämpfe. Drum lache ich eurem Drohen: der Ring
bleibt mein, und so werfe ich das Leben hinter mich.« (Er hebt eine Erdscholle auf, und wirft sie über sein Haupt hinter sich.) — Die Frauen verspot-
ten nun Siegfried, der sich so stark und weise wähne, als er blind und unfrei
sei. »Eide hat er gebrochen und weiß es nicht: ein Gut, höher und werther als
der Ring, hat er verloren, und weiß es nicht: Runen und Zauber sind ihm
gelehrt, und er hat sie vergessen. Lebe wohl, Siegfried! Ein stolzes Weib kennen wir; die wird den Ring noch heute erwerben, wenn du erschlagen bist: zu
ihr! Sie giebt uns besseres Gehör.« — Siegfried sieht ihnen lachend nach, wie
sie singend davon ziehen. Er ruft: »wär' ich nicht Gudrun treu, eine von euch
hätte ich mir gebändigt!« Er vernimmt die näher kommenden Jagdgenossen
und stößt in sein Horn, die Jäger, — Gunther und Hagen an ihrer Spitze, —
versammeln sich um Siegfried. Das Jagdmahl wird eingenommen: Siegfried, in
ausgelassener Heiterkeit, verspottet sich über sein unbelohntes Jagen: nur

entices Gunther with the idea of gaining the ring of the Nibelungs, which Siegfried would give up only in death. Gunther agrees. Hagen advises a hunt for the next day, during which Siegfried could be attacked and the murder might even be kept from Gudrun. Gunther was concerned about her. Brünnhild's desire for vengeance is sharpened by her jealousy of Gudrun. Thus the three decide on Siegfried's murder. — Siegfried appears with Gudrun, dressed for the festival, in the hall and invites the others to take part in the sacrifices to the gods and the marriage feast. The conspirators obey hypocritically. Siegfried and Gudrun are glad of the apparent return of peace.

The following morning Siegfried finds himself, in the process of pursuing game, alone in a rocky gorge along the Rhine. Three mermaids emerge from the water: they are the prophetic daughters of the depths, from whom Alberich once stole the pure Rheingold in order to forge from it the powerful, fateful ring. The curse and power of this ring would be destroyed if he gave it back to the water and thus let it be reduced to its original, pure element. The women desire the ring and beg for it from Siegfried, who refuses. (He has innocently taken on the guilt of the gods. He suffers for their injustice through his stubbornness and independence.) They announce to him disaster and the curse that is attached to the ring: he should, they say, toss it into the water, otherwise he would die that day. Siegfried: "You cunning women won't be able to trick me out of my power. The curse and your threats I don't count worth a single hair. Whatever my courage drives me to do, that is my eternal law. And what I do according to my thinking, that is what is fated for me. Whether you call this curse or blessing, I follow it and do not struggle against my power." The women: "Do you want to surpass the gods?" Siegfried: "If you showed me the possibility of defeating the gods, I would have to fight against them with my courage. I know three wiser women than you who know where the gods will one day have to fight in fearful anxiety. It is to the gods' advantage if they make sure that, when that day comes, I fight alongside them. Therefore I laugh at your threats. The ring remains mine, and thus I toss my life behind me." (He picks up a clod of dirt and tosses it over his head behind him.) — The women ridicule Siegfried, who thinks himself just as strong and wise as he is blind and unfree. "He has broken oaths and does not know it. He has lost a possession higher and worth more than the ring, and doesn't know it. He has been taught runes and magic and has forgotten them. Farewell Siegfried. We know a proud woman who will gain the ring today when you are killed. To her! She will give us a better audience." — Siegfried looks after them laughing as they depart singing. He calls out: "If I were not true to Gudrun, I would have tamed one of you!" He hears the approaching fellow hunters and sounds his horn. The hunters — Gunther and Hagen ahead of the others — crowd around Siegfried. The hunting feast is eaten. Siegfried, in relaxed good humor, ridicules himself for his unrewarded hunting. Only

Wasserwild habe sich ihm geboten, auf dessen Jagd er leider nicht gerüstet gewesen, sonst würde er seinen Genossen drei wilde Wasservögel gebracht haben, die ihm geweissagt, er würde heute noch sterben. Hagen nimmt beim Trinken die scherzhafte Weise auf: ob er denn wirklich der Vögel Gesang und Sprache verstehe? — Gunther ist trüb und schweigsam. Siegfried will ihn aufheitern und erzählt in Liedern von seiner Jugend: sein Abenteuer mit Mime, die Erlegung des Wurmes, und wie er dazugekommen, die Vögel zu verstehen. In der folgerecht geleiteten Erinnerung kommt ihm auch der Zuruf der Vögel bei, Brünnhilde aufzusuchen, die ihm beschieden sei; wie er dann zu dem flammenden Felsen gezogen und Brünnhild erweckt habe. Die Erinnerung dämmert immer heller in ihm auf. Zwei Raben fliegen jäh über sein Haupt dahin. Hagen unterbricht Siegfried: »was sagen dir diese Raben?« Siegfried fährt heftig auf. Hagen: »ich verstand sie, sie eilen, dich Wotan anzumelden«. Er stößt seinen Speer in Siegfried's Rücken. Gunther, durch Siegfried's Erzählung auf den richtigen Zusammenhang der unbegreiflichen Vorgänge mit Brünnhilde gerathend, und plötzlich daraus Siegfried's Unschuld erkennend, war, Siegfried zu retten, Hagen in den Arm gefallen, ohne jedoch den Stoß aufhalten zu können. Siegfried erhebt seinen Schild, um Hagen damit zu zerschmettern, ihn verläßt die Kraft und krachend stürzt er zusammen. Hagen hat sich abgewandt, Gunther und die Mannen umstehen in theilnahmsvoller Erschütterung Siegfried, welcher seine Augen noch einmal leuchtend aufschlägt: »Brünnhild! Brünnhild! Du strahlendes Wotanskind! Wie seh' ich hell und leuchtend dich mir nah'n! Mit heilig ernstem Lächeln sattelst du dein Roß, das thautriefend durch die Lüfte schreitet: zu mir richtest du den Lauf, hier giebt es Wal zu küren! Mich Glücklichen, den du zum Gatten korst, mich leite nun nach Walhall, daß ich zu aller Helden Ehre Allvaters Meth mag trinken, den du, strahlende Wunschmaid, mir reichest! Brünnhild! Brünnhild! Sei gegrüßt!« Er stirbt. Die Mannen erheben die Leiche auf den Schild, und geleiten sie, Gunther voran, feierlich über die Felsenhöhe von dannen.

In den Hallen der Gibichungen, deren Vorplatz im Hintergrunde auf das Rheinufer ausgeht, wird die Leiche niedergesetzt: Hagen hat mit grellem Rufe Gudrun herausgerufen, — ein wilder Eber habe ihren Gatten zerfleischt. — Gudrun stürzt voll Entsetzen über Siegfried's Leiche hin: sie klagt die Brüder des Mordes an; Gunther weist auf Hagen: er sei der wilde Eber, der Mörder Siegfried's. Hagen: »nun denn, habe ich ihn erlegt, an den kein Anderer sich wohl wagte, so ist, was sein ist, auch meine gute Beute. Der Ring ist mein!« Gunther tritt ihm entgegen: »Schamloser Albensohn, mein ist der Ring, denn von Brünnhilden war er mir bestimmt: Ihr hörtet es Alle!« — Hagen und Gunther streiten: Gunther fällt. Hagen will der Leiche den Ring entziehen, sie hebt drohend die Hand empor; Hagen weicht entsetzt zurück; Gudrun schreit in Jammer laut auf; — da tritt Brünnhild feierlich dazwischen: »Schweigt euren Jammer, eure eitle Wuth! Hier steht sein Weib, das ihr Alle verriethet!

waterfowl offered themselves to him, he says, and he was unfortunately not prepared to hunt them, otherwise he would have brought his companions three wild water birds, who predicted that he would die before day's end. As they drink, Hagen takes up the joking tone and asks if he can really understand the speech and song of the birds? — Gunther is depressed and taciturn. Siegfried wishes to cheer him up and tells about his youth in song: his adventures with Mime, the killing of the dragon, and how he came to understand the birds. As his memory is led through the events as they happened, he comes to the point where the birds advised him to seek Brünnhild, who had been granted to him; how he had then gone to the flaming rock and awakened Brünnhild. The memory returns to him more and more. Two ravens fly startlingly over his head. Hagen interrupts Siegfried to ask: "what do these ravens tell you?" Siegfried springs up violently. Hagen: "I understood them. They hurry to announce you to Wotan." He thrusts his spear into Siegfried's back. Gunther, tracing through Siegfried's narrative the correct connection of the unimaginable events concerning Brünnhilde and recognizing suddenly Siegfried's innocence, throws himself onto Hagen's arm in order to save Siegfried, but cannot stop the blow. Siegfried raises his shield in order to crush Hagen, but his strength leaves him and he falls crashing to the ground. Hagen has turned away; Gunther and the vassals surround Siegfried in shock and sympathy, who once again opens his eyes brightly: "Brünnhild! Brünnhild! You radiant child of Wotan! How I see you now, bright and shining, coming to me! With a holy, serious smile you saddle your steed, which, dripping with dew, gallops through the air. You guide him toward me. Here you can choose the slain! Now you can lead me, the fortunate one whom you chose as husband, to Valhalla, so that I can drink mead to honor all the heroes, mead that you — radiant wish-maiden — bring to me! Brünnhild! Brünnhild! My greetings to you!" He dies. The vassals raise the corpse onto his shield and accompany it, with Gunther in front, solemnly over the rocky heights.

In the hall of the Gibichungs, whose front faces the Rhine in the background, the corpse is set down. Hagen summons Gudrun with a coarse call — a wild boar has killed her husband. — Gudrun throws herself full of horror onto Siegfried's body. She accuses her brother of murder. Gunther points to Hagen; he is the wild boar, the murderer of Siegfried. Hagen: "Now then, I have felled him, against whom no other man dared. Thus what was his, is also my rightful booty. The ring is mine!" Gunther confronts him: "Shameless son of an elf. The ring is mine because it was assigned to me by Brünnhild. All of you heard it!" — Hagen and Gunther fight: Gunther falls. Hagen goes to take the ring from the corpse, and it raises its hand threateningly. Hagen springs back in shock. Gudrun cries out in misery. — At this point Brünnhilde solemnly steps between them: "Silence your grief, your idle rage! Here stands his wife, whom you all betrayed!

Nun fordre ich mein Recht, denn was geschehen sollte, ist geschehen!« —
Gudrun: »Ach, Unheilvolle! Du warst es, die uns Verderben brachte«.
Brünnhild: »Armselige, schweig'! Du warst nur seine Buhlerin: sein Gemahl
bin ich, der er Eide geschworen, noch eh' er je dich sah«. Gudrun: »Weh' mir!
Verfluchter Hagen, was riethest du mir mit dem Trank, durch den ich' ihr den
Gatten stahl: denn nun weiß ich, daß er Brünnhild nur durch den Trank
vergaß«. Brünnhild: »O, er war rein! Nie wurden Eide treuer gehalten, als
durch ihn. So hat ihn Hagen nun nicht erschlagen, nein, für Wotan zeichnete
er ihn, zu dem ich ihn nun geleiten soll. Jetzt hab' auch ich gebüßt; rein und
frei bin ich: denn Er, der Herrliche nur, hatte mich gezwungen.« Sie läßt am
Ufer Scheithaufen errichten, Siegfried's Leiche zu verbrennen: kein Roß, kein
Knecht soll mit ihm geopfert werden, sie allein will zu seiner Ehre ihren Leib
den Göttern darbringen. Zuvor nimmt sie ihr Erbe in Besitz; der Tarnhelm
soll mit verbrennen: den Ring aber steckt sie selbst an. »Du übermüthiger
Held, wie hieltest du mich gebannt! All mein Wissen verrieth ich dir, dem
Sterblichen, und mußte so meiner Weisheit verlustig sein; du nütztest es nicht,
auf dich allein nur verließest du dich: nun du es frei geben mußtest durch den
Tod, kommt mir mein Wissen wieder, und dieses Ringes Runen erkenne ich.
Des Urgesetzes Runen kenn' ich nun auch, der Nornen alten Spruch! Hört
denn, ihr herrlichen Götter, euer Unrecht ist getilgt: dankt ihm, dem Helden,
der eure Schuld auf sich nahm. Er gab es nun in meine Hand, das Werk zu
vollenden: gelöset sei der Nibelungen Knechtschaft, der Ring soll sie nicht
mehr binden. Nicht soll ihn Alberich empfangen; der soll nicht mehr euch
knechten; dafür sei er aber selbst auch frei wie ihr. Denn diesen Ring stelle ich
euch zu, weise Schwestern der Wassertiefe; die Gluth, die mich verbrennt, soll
das böse Kleinod reinigen; ihr löset es auf und bewahret es harmlos, das
Rheingold, das euch geraubt, um Knechtschaft und Unheil daraus zu schmieden. Nur Einer herrsche, Allvater, herrlicher, du! Daß ewig deine Macht sei,
führ' ich dir diesen zu: empfange ihn wohl, er ist dess' werth!« — Unter
feierlichen Gesängen schreitet Brünnhild auf den Scheithaufen zu Siegfried's
Leiche. Gudrun ist über den erschlagenen Gunther, in tiefen Schmerz aufgelöst, hingebeugt im Vordergrunde. Die Flammen sind über Brünnhild und
Siegfried zusammengeschlagen: — plötzlich leuchtet es im hellsten Glanze
auf: über einem düstern Wolkensaume erhebt sich der Glanz, in welchem Brünnhild, im Waffenschmuck zu Roß, als Walküre Siegfried an der
Hand von dannen geleitet. Zugleich schwellen die Uferwellen des Rheines bis
an den Eingang der Halle an: die drei Wasserfrauen entführen auf ihnen den
Ring und den Helm. Hagen stürzt wie wahnsinnig auf sie zu, das Kleinod
ihnen zu entreißen, — die Frauen erfassen ihn und ziehen ihn mit sich in die
Tiefe hinab.

Now I demand my right, for what had to happen, has happened."
Gudrun: "Ah! Bringer of misfortune! It was you who brought us all ruin."
Brünnhild: "Poor thing, be silent! You were only his paramour. I am his
wife, to whom he swore oaths before he ever saw you." Gudrun: "Woe is
me! Accursed Hagen, why did you advise the drink through which I stole
her husband? For now I know that he forgot Brünnhild only through that
drink." Brünnhild: "Oh, he was pure! Never were oaths kept better than
by him. Hagen did not strike him down, no, he marked him for Wotan,
to whom I shall now lead him. Now I have also suffered for it. I am pure
and free. For He alone, the Lordly one had me in his power." She has a
great pyre built along the river bank to burn Siegfried's body. No horse,
no servant should be sacrificed along with him; she alone will bring her
body to the gods to honor him. But first she takes possession of her in-
heritance; the tarnhelm should burn up with everything else: the ring she
puts on her own finger. "You exuberant hero, how you held me in your
spell! All of my wisdom, I passed on to you, the mortal, and thus had to
lose it all. You did not use it. You depended on yourself alone. Now that
you had to give it away through your death, the wisdom returns to me and
I recognize the runes on this ring. I now also recognize the runes of the
original law, the ancient lore of the Norns! Hear now, you lordly gods;
your injustice has been erased. Thank him, the hero, who took your
guilt upon himself. He gave it now into my hand to finish the task. Let the
slavery of the Nibelungs be over; the ring shall no longer bind them.
Alberich will not receive it. He shall no longer hold you as slaves. But he
himself will now be free like you. For I shall now return this ring to you,
wise sisters of the depths. The fire that burns me will also purify the evil
jewel. You will melt it down and keep it harmless, the Rheingold, which was
stolen from you so that slavery and misfortune could be forged from it. Let
only One rule, All-father, lordly one, you! So that your power will be
eternal, I bring this man to you. Receive him well: he is worthy of it!" —
Accompanied by solemn songs, Brünnhild advances to the pyre and Siegfried's corpse. Gudrun remains bowed over Gunther's body, dissolved in
deep pain, in the foreground. The flames close over Brünnhild and Siegfried. — Suddenly a bright light arises. The light arises over a dark bank of
clouds in which Brünnhild as Valkyrie, in armor on her steed, leads Siegfried
by the hand. At the same time the waves of the Rhine swell to the entrance
of the hall. The three mermaids carry the ring and the tarnhelm away on the
waves. Hagen leaps like a madman after them in an attempt to snatch the
jewel from them — the mermaids seize him and pull him down with them
into the depths.

Siegfried's Tod / Siegfried's Death

Commentary

WAGNER THOUGHT ENOUGH OF HIS *Siegfried's Tod,* written in November 1848, to include it in his collected works in a form close to its original. The published text was translated into English by William Ashton Ellis and included in 1899 as part of the final volume of his *Richard Wagner's Prose Works.*[1] Wagner's verse is generally understandable, if ornate and occasionally ponderous, but a translation should not be more difficult to read than the original. Ashton Ellis felt called upon to try to match, if not exceed, Wagner's stylistic excesses in his translations, and the results are sometimes impenetrable. As an example, here is a short passage from Alberich's speech to Hagen near the beginning of act 2 in Wagner's original:

> dich Unverzagten zeugt' ich mir selbst,
> du, Hagen, hältst mir Treu'!
> Doch wie stark du bist,
> nicht ließ ich den Wurm dich besteh'n

Ashton Ellis rendered the lines this way:

> Thee, changeless one, begat I myself;
> Thou, Hagen, troth wilt cherish!
> Yet, strong though thy thews
> The Worm I durst not let thee strike (22)

Wagner's German is clarity itself next to Ashton Ellis's "English."

With the goal of translating simply what Wagner wrote, I have tried to maintain a line-by-line correspondence, but it has not always worked, and some pairs of lines have fallen victim to the differences between (Wagner's) German and English syntax. The result is certainly not singable, nor does it set out to provide a truly poetic text, but it should fulfill its purpose of informing the serious student of Wagner's *Ring* where the journey to *Der Ring des Nibelungen* began, just as the composer intended when he published this early version of the drama.

As I have already mentioned, Wagner wrote musical sketches for the earliest parts of *Siegfried's Tod,* but he needed the theoretical underpinnings he would work out in the pages of *Oper und Drama,* the most important of his

---

[1] Vol. 8 (Reprint, New York: Broude Brothers, 1966), 1–52. I am not aware of a more recent translation.

theoretical writings during the early Zurich period, before he could produce something usable in the new musical language he invented for the *Ring*. Even then, it took him several years to work out the textual changes that would later find their way into *Der Ring des Nibelungen*. He realized that the backstory was simply too large to be included in the backward-looking passages of his Siegfried opera, and he attempted to clarify things with a second opera, dealing with Siegfried's youth, which he called *Der junge Siegfried*. Finally he realized the need for additional prequels and wrote the poems for *Das Rheingold* and *Die Walküre*. When these projects were completed, he went back and revised *Der junge Siegfried* and *Siegfried's Tod* to agree with them, privately printing the texts for the whole cycle in 1853. His sketchbooks show that he was working on musical ideas for the *Ring* before then, but he actually began work on the mammoth task of composition in November 1853. He retained the titles *Der junge Siegfried* and *Siegfried's Tod* for the last two operas of the cycle until 1856, when he first mentioned the present titles: *Siegfried* and *Götterdämmerung*, titles he used for the first public printing of the text in 1863.[2]

It is worth noting that even after transforming the story into the four-part *Der Ring des Nibelungen*, Wagner retained in *Götterdämmerung*[3] the dramatic structure he had originally designed for *Siegfried's Tod* with only one real addition: the passage known as Hagen's Watch was inserted to cover the scene change at the end of act 1, scene 2. In the commentary following the translation I will consider each of the scenic units in the work. In the German text of *Siegfried's Tod* that I provide here (which is taken verbatim from the *Gesammelte Schriften*) I have italicized all the lines that survive unchanged (or virtually unchanged) in *Götterdämmerung*.

[2] Barry Millington, *Wagner* (Princeton, NJ: Princeton UP, 1984), 196.

[3] References to *Götterdämmerung* are to the text and translation by Stewart Spencer in *Wagner's Ring of the Nibelung: A Companion*, ed. Stewart Spencer and Barry Millington (New York: Thames and Hudson, 1993), 277–351.

Siegfried's Tod / Siegfried's Death

Personen/Cast of Characters.

SIEGFRIED.

GUNTHER.

HAGEN.

ALBERICH.

BRÜNNHILDE.

GUDRUNE.

DREI NORNEN. (THREE NORNS)

DREI WASSERFRAUEN. (THREE MERMAIDS)

WALKÜREN. (VALKYRIES)

Am Rhein (On the Rhine).

Vorspiel.

(Nach sehr kurzer musikalischer Vorbereitung wird der Vorhang aufgezogen. Die Bühne stellt den Gipfel eines Felsenberges dar: links der Eingang eines natürlichen Steingemaches. Der Saum der Höhe ist nach dem Hintergrunde zu ganz frei: rechts hohe Tannen. — Helle Sternennacht.)

DIE DREI NORNEN.
(hohe Frauengestalten in dunklen, faltigen Gewändern, spannen ein goldenes Seil aus. Die Erste [Älteste] knüpft das Seil, zur äußersten Seite rechts, an einer Tanne fest. Die Zweite [Jüngere] windet es links um einen Stein. Die Dritte [Jüngste] hält das Ende in der Mitte des Hintergrundes.)
DIE ERSTE NORN.
     In Osten wob ich.
DIE ZWEITE.
     In Westen wand ich.
DIE DRITTE.
     Nach Norden werf' ich.

(Zur Zweiten.)

     Was wandest du im Westen?
DIE ZWEITE.
(zur Ersten.)
     Was wobest du im Osten?
DIE ERSTE.
(während sie das Seil von der Tanne löst.)
     Rheingold raubte Alberich,
     schmiedete einen Ring,
     band durch ihn seine Brüder.
DIE ZWEITE.
(das Seil vom Stein loswindend.)
     Knechte die Nibelungen,
     Knecht auch Alberich,
     da ihm der Ring geraubt.
DIE DRITTE.
(das Ende des Seiles nach dem äußersten Hintergrunde zuwerfend.)
     Frei die Schwarzalben,
     frei auch Alberich:
     Rheingold ruh' in der Tiefe!

Prologue

(After a very short musical preparation the curtain is raised. The stage shows the summit of a rocky mountain: on the left the entrance to a natural stone chamber. The horizon is completely open toward the rear: on the right there are high fir trees. — Bright starry night.)

THE THREE NORNS
(Tall female figures in dark, flowing robes, stretch a golden rope. The First [eldest] ties the rope, on the extreme right side, to a fir tree. The Second [younger] winds it on the left side around a stone. The Third [youngest] holds the end in the middle of the background.)
THE FIRST NORN
  In the east I wove it.
THE SECOND
  In the west I wound it.
THE THIRD
  To the north I toss it.

(To the Second.)

  What did you wind in the west?
THE SECOND
(to the First)
  What did you weave in the east?
THE FIRST
(while loosening the rope from the fir tree)
  Alberich stole the Rheingold,
  Forged a ring,
  Bound his brothers with it.
THE SECOND
(unwinding the rope from the stone)
  The Nibelungs are slaves,
  Alberich is also a slave,
  Since the ring was stolen from him.
THE THIRD
(tossing the end of the rope into the farthest background)
  Free are the black-elves,
  Alberich is also free:
  Let the Rheingold rest in the deeps!

(Sie wirft das Seil der Zweiten, diese es wieder der Ersten zu, welche es von Neuem wieder an die Tanne knüpft.)

DIE ERSTE.
　　In Osten wob ich.
DIE ZWEITE.
(die das Seil wieder um den Stein gewunden.)
　　In Westen wand ich.
DIE DRITTE.
(das Ende wieder emporhaltend.)
　　Nach Norden werf' ich. —
　　Was wandest du im Westen?
DIE ZWEITE.
　　Was wobest du im Osten?
DIE ERSTE
(das Seil wieder lösend.)
　　Der Götter Burg bauten Riesen,
　　begehrten drohend zum Dank den Ring:
　　Ihn entrissen die Götter dem Nibelung.
DIE ZWEITE.
(das Seil wieder loswindend.)
　　Sorgen seh' ich die Götter,
　　es grollt in Banden die Tiefe:
　　Freie nur geben Frieden.
DIE DRITTE.
(das Ende wieder werfend.)
　　Freudig trotzet ein Froher,
　　frei für die Götter zu streiten:
　　durch Sieg bringt Friede ein Held.

(Sie verfahren mit dem Seil genau wieder wie zuvor.)

DIE ERSTE.
　　In Osten wob ich.
DIE ZWEITE.
　　In Westen wand ich.
DIE DRITTE.
　　Nach Norden werf' ich. —
　　Was wandest du im Westen?
DIE ZWEITE.
　　Was wobest du im Osten?
DIE ERSTE.
　　Einen Wurm zeugten die Riesen,

(She tosses the rope to the Second, who tosses it to the First, who ties it anew to the fir tree.)

THE FIRST
    In the east I wove it.
THE SECOND
(who has wound the rope again around the stone)
    In the west I wound it.
THE THIRD
(holding up the end again)
    To the north I toss it. —
    What did you wind in the west?
THE SECOND
    What did you weave in the east?
THE FIRST
(loosening the rope again)
    Giants built the gods' castle,
    Demanded as thanks the ring:
    The gods stole it from the Nibelung.
THE SECOND
(unwinding the rope again)
    I see the gods in concern,
    Those in the depths groan in bondage:
    Free men alone give peace.
THE THIRD
(tossing the end again)
    Joyfully a happy man sets out
    To fight freely for the gods:
    Through victory the hero brings peace.

(They repeat their actions with the rope as before.)

THE FIRST
    In the east I wove it.
THE SECOND
    In the west I wound it.
THE THIRD
    To the north I toss it. —
    What did you wind in the west?
THE SECOND
    What did you weave in the east?
THE FIRST
    The giants conceived a dragon,

des Ringes würgenden Hüter.
Siegfried hat ihn erschlagen.
DIE ZWEITE.
Brünnhild gewann der Held,
brach der Walküre Schlaf:
liebend lehrt sie ihm Runen.
DIE DRITTE.
Der Runen nicht achtend, untreu auf Erden,
treu doch auf ewig, trügt er die Edle:
doch seine That taugt sie zu deuten,
frei zu vollenden, was froh er begann.

(Sie werfen sich das Seil wieder zu.)

Windest du noch im Westen?
DIE ZWEITE.
Webest du noch im Osten?

(Morgendämmerung bricht an.)

DIE ERSTE.
Meinem Brunnen nahet sich Wotan.
DIE ZWEITE.
Sein Auge neigt sich zum Quell.
DIE DRITTE.
Weise Antwort laßt ihm werden!
DIE DREI NORNEN ZUSAMMEN.
(während sie das Seil vollständig aufwinden.)
Schließet das Seil, wahret es wohl!
Was wir spannen, bindet die Welt.

(Sie umfassen sich und entschweben dem Felsen. — Der Tag bricht an. —
Siegfried und Brünnhilde treten aus dem Steingemach. Siegfried ist in vollen
Waffen; Brünnhilde führt ein Roß am Zaume.)

BRÜNNHILDE.
Zu neuen Thaten, theurer Helde,
wie lieb' ich dich — ließ' ich dich nicht?
Ein einzig Sorgen macht mich säumen,
daß dir zu wenig mein Werth gewann.
Was Götter mich wiesen, gab ich dir,
heiliger Runen reichen Hort;
doch meiner Stärke magdlichen Stamm

The strangling keeper of the ring,
Siegfried slew it.
THE SECOND
The hero won Brünnhild
Broke the sleep of the Valkyrie:
Lovingly she taught him runes.
THE THIRD
Not heeding the runes, untrue on the earth,
But true for eternity, he deceives the noble woman
But she can understand his deed,
And freely complete what he began in joy.

(They toss the rope again.)

Are you still winding in the west?
THE SECOND
Are you still weaving in the east?

(Dawn breaks.)

THE FIRST
Wotan approaches my spring.
THE SECOND
His eye looks down at the water.
THE THIRD
Let him receive wise answers!
THE THREE NORNS TOGETHER
(while they wind up the rope completely)
Secure the rope, protect it well!
That which we tie, binds the world.

(They embrace and rise from the rock. — Day breaks — Siegfried and
Brünnhilde come out of the stone chamber. Siegfried is fully armed;
Brünnhilde leads a horse by its bridle.)

BRÜNNHILDE
To new deeds, dear hero,
how would I love you — if I did not let you go?
A single worry causes me to hesitate,
That you have gained too little of my power.
What the gods taught me, I gave to you,
The rich hoard of holy runes,
But the hero to whom I now bow

nahm mir der Held, dem ich nun mich neige:
des Wissens bar, doch des Wunsches voll,
an Liebe reich, doch ledig der Kraft —
mög'st du die Arme nicht verachten,
die dir nur gönnen, nicht geben mehr kann.

SIEGFRIED.

Mehr gabst du Wunderfrau,
als ich zu wahren weiß:
nicht zürne, wenn dein Lehren
mich unbelehret ließ!
Ein Wissen doch wahr' ich wohl:
daß mir Brünnhilde lebt;
eine Lehre lernt' ich leicht:
Brünnhilde's zu gedenken.

BRÜNNHILDE.

Willst du mir Minne schenken,
gedenke deiner nur,
gedenke deiner Thaten!
Gedenke des wilden Feuers,
das furchtlos du durchschrittest,
da den Felsen es rings umbrann.

SIEGFRIED.

Brünnhilde zu gewinnen!

BRÜNNHILDE.

Gedenk' der beschildeten Frau,
die in tiefem Schlafe du fandest,
der den festen Helm du erbrachst.

SIEGFRIED.

Brünnhilde zu erwecken!

BRÜNNHILDE.

Gedenk' der Eide — die uns einen,
gedenk' der Treue — die wir tragen,
gedenk' der Liebe — der wir leben:
Brünnhilde's dann vergißt du nicht.

SIEGFRIED.

Den Ring ich dir nun reiche
zum Tausche deiner Runen:
was der Thaten je ich schuf,
dess' Tugend schließet er ein.
Ich erschlug einen wilden Wurm,
der grimmig lang ihn bewacht:
nun wahre du seine Kraft
als Weihegruß meiner Treu'.

Took away the maidenly source of my strength,:
Deprived of lore, but full of desire,
Rich in love, but the power is lost —
Please do not despise the poor woman
Who can grant, but give nothing more.

SIEGFRIED

Miraculous woman, you have given more
Than I know how to keep:
Do not be angry, if your lessons
Have left me untaught!
One thing I do know well:
That Brünnhilde lives for me;
One lesson I learned easily:
To remember Brünnhilde.

BRÜNNHILDE

If you wish to give me love,
Remember yourself only,
Remember your deeds!
Remember the wild fire
Which you fearlessly crossed,
When it burned around this rock.

SIEGFRIED

To win Brünnhilde!

BRÜNNHILDE

Remember the woman under the shield,
Whom you found in deepest sleep,
Whose strong helmet you broke open.

SIEGFRIED

To awaken Brünnhilde!

BRÜNNHILDE

Remember the oaths — that bind us,
Remember the fidelity — that we bear,
Remember the love — for which we live:
Then you will not forget Brünnhilde.

SIEGFRIED

I present you now with the Ring
In exchange for your runes:
Whatever deeds I have accomplished
It contains their virtues.
I killed a wild dragon,
Which had long watched over it:
Now you protect its power
As a holy greeting of my fidelity!

BRÜNNHILDE.
>*Ihn geiz' ich als einziges Gut, —*
>drum *nimm nun auch* Grane, *mein Roß!*
>*Ging sein Lauf mit mir einst kühn durch die Lüfte, —*
>*mit mir verlor er die* hehre *Art;*
>*über Wolken hin auf blitzenden Wettern*
>die alten Wege nicht führt er mehr.
>Dir, Helde, soll er nun gehorchen:
>*nie ritt ein Recke edleres Roß!*
>*Du hüt' ihn wohl, er hört dein Wort:*
>*o bring'* ihm *oft Brünnhilde's Gruß!*

SIEGFRIED.
>*Durch deine Tugend allein*
>*soll so ich Thaten noch wirken!*
>*Meine Kämpfe kiesest du,*
>*meine Siege kehren zu dir!*
>*Auf deines Rosses Rücken,*
>*in deines Schildes Schirm —*
>*nicht Siegfried* bin *ich mehr,*
>*bin nur Brünnhilde's Arm!*

BRÜNNHILDE.
>*O, wär' Brünnhild deine Seele!*

SIEGFRIED.
>*Durch sie entbrennt mir der Muth.*

BRÜNNHILDE.
>*So wärst du Siegfried und Brünnhild?*

SIEGFRIED.
>Wohin ich geh' ziehen *Beide.*

BRÜNNHILDE.
>*So verödet mein Felsensaal?*

SIEGFRIED.
>*Vereint faßt er uns Zwei.*

BRÜNNHILDE.
>*O heil'ge Götter! Hehre Geschlechter!*
>*Weidet eur' Aug' an dem weihvollen Paar!*
>*Getrennt — wer* mag *es scheiden!*
>*Geschieden — trennt es sich* nicht!
>Heil dir, Siegfried! Glanz der Welt!
>Heil! Heil! Wonne der Götter!

SIEGFRIED.
>*Heil dir, Brünnhild! Strahlender Stern!*
>Heil! Heil! Sonne der Helden!

BRÜNNHILDE

> I desire it as my only possession, —
> So take now Grane my steed!
> Once he flew boldly with me through the air —
> With me he lost the magical skill;
> He no longer travels the old ways,
> Over clouds through lightning and wind.
> He should now obey you, Hero,
> Never a warrior rode a nobler steed!
> Protect him well, he obeys your word:
> O bring him often Brünnhilde's greeting!

SIEGFRIED

> Through your virtues alone
> Shall I now accomplish deeds!
> You chose my battles
> My victories return to you!
> On your steed's back,
> In your shield's protection —
> I am no longer Siegfried,
> I am only Brünnhilde's arm.

BRÜNNHILDE

> O, if only Brünnhilde were your soul!

SIEGFRIED

> Through her my courage is enflamed.

BRÜNNHILDE

> So you would be both Siegfried and Brünnhild'?

SIEGFRIED

> Wherever I go, both shall go.

BRÜNNHILDE

> So my rocky hall will be deserted?

SIEGFRIED

> United it holds us both.

BRÜNNHILDE

> O holy gods! Holy races!
> Let your eyes gaze on this blessed pair!
> Separated — who can part them!
> Parted — they cannot be separated!
> Hail to you, Siegfried, Glory of the world!
> Hail! Hail! Joy of the gods!

SIEGFRIED

> Hail to you, Brünnhilde! Shining star!
> Hail! Hail! Sun of heroes!

BEIDE.

> *Heil! Heil!*

(Siegfried leitet das Roß den Felsen hinab, Brünnhilde blickt ihm entzückt lange nach. Aus der Tiefe hört man dann Siegfried's Horn munter ertönen. — Der Vorhang fällt.

Das Orchester nimmt die Weise des Hornes auf und führt sie in einem kräftigen Satze durch. — Darauf beginnt sogleich der erste Akt.)

Erster Akt.

(Die Halle der Gibichungen am Rhein: sie ist nach dem Hintergrunde zu ganz offen; diesen nimmt ein freier Uferraum bis zum Flusse hin ein: felsige Anhöhen umgränzen den Raum.)

Erste Scene.

(Gunther und Gudrune auf dem Hochsitze; davor ein Tisch mit Trinkgeräth, an welchem Hagen sitzt.)

GUNTHER.

> *Nun* sag', *Hagen*, unfroher *Helde!*
> *Sitze ich* stark *am Rhein*
> zu der Gibichungen *Ruhm?*

HAGEN.

> *Dich ächten* Gibichung *acht' ich zu neiden:*
> *Frau Grimhild* lehrt' es mich schon,
> *die beide uns gebar.*

GUNTHER.

> *Dich neide ich — nicht neide mich du!*
> *Erbte ich Erstlings*macht,
> *Weisheit ward dir allein.*
> *Halbbrüder Zwist* nie zähmte sich *besser:*
> *Deinem Rath nur* zoll' ich *Lob,*
> *frag' ich dich nach meinem Ruhm.*

HAGEN.

> *So schelt' ich den Rath, da schlecht noch dein Ruhm,*

BOTH
    Hail! Hail!

(Siegfried leads the horse down the rocks, Brünnhild gazes longingly after him. From the depths Siegfried's horn is heard joyfully sounding. — The curtain falls.
The orchestra takes up the horn's melody and develops it in a powerful movement. — Then the first act begins without a pause.)

First Act

(The hall of the Gibichungs on the Rhine: it is completely open toward the background, which encompasses a free open space down to the river: rocky heights enclose the space.)

First Scene.

(Gunther and Gudrune on the high seat; in front of this a table with drinking vessels, where Hagen is sitting.)

GUNTHER.
    Now say, Hagen, unhappy hero!
    Do I sit mighty on the Rhine
    Bringing the Gibichungs fame?
HAGEN
    I must envy you, genuine Gibichung:
    Lady Grimhild taught me that already,
    The one who bore us both.
GUNTHER
    I envy you — do not envy me!
    If I gained the power of the first-born,
    Wisdom was given to you alone.
    Half-brother friction was never better tamed:
    I give praise to your counsel alone,
    When I ask you about my fame.
HAGEN
    So I curse my advice, because your fame is weak,

denn hohe Güter weiß ich,
die der Gibichung nicht gewann.
GUNTHER.
Verschwiegst du sie, so schelte auch ich.
HAGEN.
In sommerlicher Stärke
seh' ich den Gibichsstamm,
dich, Gunther, unbeweibt,
dich, Gudrun, ohne Mann.
GUNTHER.
Wen räthst du nun zu frei'n,
daß unserm Ruhm es fromme?
HAGEN.
Ein Weib weiß ich — das hehrste *der Welt.*
auf Felsen hoch ihr Sitz,
ein Feuer umbrennt den *Saal;*
nur wer durch das Feuer bricht,
darf Brünnhilde's Freier sein.
GUNTHER.
Vermag das mein Muth zu besteh'n?
HAGEN.
Einem Stärkern noch ist's nur bestimmt.
GUNTHER.
Wer ist der streitlichste Mann?
HAGEN.
Siegfried, der Wälsungen Sproß:
der ist der stärkste Held.
Von Wotan stammte Wälse,
von dem *ein Zwillingspaar —*
Siegmund und Siegelind:
den ächtesten Wälsung sie zeugten,
seines Vaters leibliche Schwester
gebar ihn im wilden Forst:
der dort so herrlich *erwuchs,*
den wünsch' ich Gudrunen zum Mann.
GUDRUNE.
Welche That schuf er so hehr,
daß als herrlichster Held er gepriesen?
HAGEN.
Auf Neid*haide den Niblungenhort*
bewachte ein Riesenwurm;
Siegfried schloß ihm den freislichen Schlund,
erschlug ihn mit siegendem Schwert.

> For I know high goods
> Which the Gibichung has not yet won.

GUNTHER

> If you keep them secret, I shall also scold.

HAGEN

> I see the heirs of Gibich
> In summery strength,
> But you, Gunther, without a wife,
> And you, Gudrun, without a husband.

GUNTHER

> Whom do you advise that I woo;
> Who will increase our fame?

HAGEN

> I know of a woman — the noblest of the world.
> Her seat is on a high rock,
> A fire surrounds her hall;
> Only the one who can break through the fire
> Can be Brünnhilde's wooer.

GUNTHER

> Can my courage accomplish that?

HAGEN

> It is only fated for a stronger man.

GUNTHER

> Who is that mightiest man?

HAGEN

> Siegfried, the scion of the Volsungs:
> He is the strongest hero.
> Volsung was Wotan's son,
> A pair of twins came from him —
> Siegmund and Siegelind:
> They conceived the most genuine Volsung
> His father's twin sister
> Bore him in the wild forest:
> The one who grew up so magnificently there,
> Him I wish as a husband for Gudrun.

GUDRUNE

> What kind of noble deed did he accomplish,
> That he is praised as highest of heroes?

HAGEN

> On Neidhaide the Niblung's treasure
> Was guarded by a giant dragon:
> Siegfried closed his frightening gorge,
> Killed him with his victorious sword.

Solch' ungeheurer That
er*tagte des Helden Ruhm.*

GUNTHER.

Von der *Niblungen Hort vernahm ich;*
er hütet *den reichsten Schatz?*

HAGEN.

Wer wohl ihn zu nützen weiß,
dem neigte sich wahrlich die Welt.

GUNTHER.

Und Siegfried hat ihn erkämpft?

HAGEN.

Knecht sind die Niblungen ihm.

GUNTHER.

Und Brünnhild gewänne nur Er?

HAGEN.

Sie möchte kein Andrer besteh'n.

GUNTHER.

(sich unwillig erhebend.)

Nun zeigst du böse Art!
Was ich nicht zwingen soll,
das lässest du mich verlangen.

HAGEN.

Gewänne sie Siegfried für dich,
wär' dann Brünnhild weniger dein?

GUNTHER.

(bewegt in der Halle hin und her schreitend.)

Was zwänge den frohen Mann
für mich die Maid zu frei'n?

HAGEN.

Ihn zwänge bald deine Bitte,
bänd' ihn Gudrune zuvor.

GUDRUNE.

Du Spötter, böser Hagen!
Wie sollt' ich Siegfried binden?
Ist er der herrlichste Held,
der Erde holdeste Frauen
friedeten längst ihn schon!

HAGEN.

Gedenk' des Trankes im Schrein,
vertrau' mir, der ihn gewann:
den Helden, den du verlangst,
bindet er liebend an dich.
Träte nun Siegfried ein, —

Such a magnificent deed
Established the hero's fame.

GUNTHER

I have heard of the Niblung's hoard;
It contains the richest treasure?

HAGEN

Whoever knew how to use it,
The world would bow to him.

GUNTHER

And Siegfried has won it?

HAGEN

The Niblungs are his servants.

GUNTHER

And only he could win Brünnhilde?

HAGEN

No other could pass the test.

GUNTHER

(rising reluctantly)
Now you show your evil character!
That which I cannot win,
You cause me to desire.

HAGEN

If Siegfried were to gain her for you,
Would Brünnhilde be less yours?

GUNTHER

(impatiently striding to and fro in the hall)
What would force the happy man
To woo the maiden for me?

HAGEN

Your request would force him,
If Gudrune were to bind him first.

GUDRUNE

You mocker, evil Hagen!
How should I bind him?
If he is the mightiest hero of the world,
Then the most desirable women of the earth
Would have won him already!

HAGEN

Remember the potion in the cabinet,
Trust me, the one who obtained it;
The hero you desire,
It will bind to you in love.
If Siegfried were now to enter —

genöss' er des würzigen Trankes, —
daß vor dir ein Weib er ersah,
daß je einem Weib er genaht, —
vergessen müßt' er das ganz. —
Nun redet: wie dünkt euch Hagen's Rath?
GUNTHER.
(der wieder an den Tisch getreten und, auf ihn gelehnt, aufmerksam zuge-
hört hat.)
Gepriesen sei Grimhilde,
die uns den Bruder gab!
GUDRUNE.
Möcht' ich Siegfried je erseh'n!
GUNTHER.
Wie suchten wir ihn auf?
HAGEN.
Jagt er auf Thaten wonnig umher,
zum engen Tann wird ihm die Welt:
wohl stürmt er in Jagens Lust
auch zu Gibich's Strand an den Rhein.
GUNTHER.
Willkommen hieß' ich ihn gern.

(Siegfried's Horn läßt sich von ferne vernehmen. — Sie lauschen.)

Vom Rhein her tönt das Horn.
HAGEN.
(ist dem Ufer zu gegangen, späht nach dem Flusse und ruft zurück.)
In einem Nachen Held und Roß!
Der bläst so munter das Horn. —
Ein selt'ner *Schlag wie von müß'ger Hand*
treibt jach den Nachen *gegen den Strom:*
so mühloser *Kraft in des Ruders* Wucht
rühmt sich nur der, der den Wurm erschlug.
Siegfried ist's, — sicher kein Andrer!
GUNTHER.
Jagt er vorbei?
HAGEN.
(durch die hohlen Hände nach dem Flusse zurufend.)
Hoiho! Wohin, du heit'rer Helde?
SIEGFRIED'S STIMME.
(aus der Ferne vom Flusse her schallend.)
Zu Gibich's starkem Sohne.

If he were to taste of the spiced potion —
He would have to forget completely
That he ever saw a woman before you —
That he had ever been near a woman.
Now speak: how do you find Hagen's advice?

GUNTHER

(who has returned to the table and, leaning on it, has listened attentively.)

Let us praise Grimhilde,
Who gave us such a brother!

GUDRUNE

If only I could ever see Siegfried!

GUNTHER

How would we find him?

HAGEN

If he hunts for deeds everywhere
The world becomes a narrow forest for him:
He may well in the pleasure of his hunt
Storm onto Gibich's shore on the Rhine.

GUNTHER

I would be happy to welcome him.

(Siegfried's Horn can be heard from the distance. — They listen.)

The horn sounds from the Rhine.

HAGEN

(has gone to the bank. He looks down the river and calls back.)

In a small boat hero and steed!
He is sounding that horn so merrily.
An occasional stroke as from an idle hand
Drives the boat swiftly against the current;
Such a careless power on the oar
Can only be wielded by the one who killed the dragon.
It is Siegfried — certainly no other!

GUNTHER

Does he rush past?

HAGEN

(cups his hands before his mouth and calls toward the river.)

Hoiho! Where are you headed, merry hero?

SIEGFRIED'S VOICE

(sounding from the distance from the direction of the river.)

To Gibich's powerful son.

HAGEN.

> *In seine Halle entbiet' ich dich.*
> *Hierher! Hier lege an! —*
> *Heil Siegfried, theurer Held!*

Zweite Scene

SIEGFRIED.
(legt an)

(Gunther ist zu Hagen an das Ufer getreten. — Gudrune erblickt Siegfried vom Hochsitze aus, heftet eine Zeit lang in freudiger Überraschung die Blicke auf ihn, und, als die Männer dann näher zur Halle schreiten, entfernt sie sich, in sichtbarer Verwirrung, links durch eine Thür in ihr Gemach.)

SIEGFRIED.
(hat sein Roß an das Land geführt und lehnt jetzt ruhig an ihm.)
> *Wer ist Gibich's Sohn?*

GUNTHER.
> *Gunther, ich — den du suchst.*

SIEGFRIED.
> *Dich hört' ich rühmen weit am Rhein:*
> *nun ficht mit mir — oder sei mein Freund!*

GUNTHER.
> *Laß den Kampf, sei willkommen!*

SIEGFRIED.
> *Wo berg' ich das Roß?*

HAGEN.
> *Ich biet' ihm Rast.*

SIEGFRIED.
> *Du riefst mich Siegfried, — sah'st du mich schon?*

HAGEN.
> *Ich kannte dich nur an deiner Kraft.*

SIEGFRIED.
> *Wohl hüte mir Grane! Du hieltest nie*
> *von edlerer Zucht am Zaume ein Roß.*

(Hagen führt das Roß rechts hinter die Halle ab und kehrt bald darauf wieder zurück.)
(Gunther schreitet mit Siegfried in die Halle vor.)

HAGEN

I invite you to his hall.
Come here! Tie up here! —
Hail Siegfried, treasured hero!

Second Scene

SIEGFRIED
(docking his boat)

(Gunther has joined Hagen on the bank — Gudrune watches Siegfried from her high seat, gazes at him for a while in joyful surprise, then, as the men approach the hall, she leaves in visible confusion to the left through a door into her chamber.)

SIEGFRIED
(has led his horse onto the bank and is quietly leaning on it)
Who is Gibich's son?
GUNTHER
Gunther, I am the one you seek.
SIEGFRIED
I heard praise for you far down the Rhine:
Now fight with me — or be my friend!
GUNTHER
Don't think of battle, be welcome!
SIEGFRIED
Where shall I leave my steed?
HAGEN
I'll offer him rest.
SIEGFRIED
You called me Siegfried — have you seen me before?
HAGEN
I recognized you from your strength.
SIEGFRIED
Take good care of Grane! You've never held
The reins of a nobler steed.

(Hagen leads the horse away behind the hall and returns almost immediately.)
(Gunther strides into the hall with Siegfried.)

GUNTHER.

Begrüße froh, o Held,
die Halle meines Vaters:
wohin du schreitest,
was du siehst, —
das achte nun dein Eigen.
Dein ist mein Erbe,
Land und Leute, —
hilf, Wotan, *meinem Eide! —*
mich selbst geb' ich zum Mann.

SIEGFRIED.

Nicht Land noch Leute biet' ich,
noch Vaters Haus und Hof:
sein einig Erbe,
Rächer's Recht —
das zehrt' ich allein schon auf.
Nur Waffen hab' ich
— selbst gewonnen —
hilf, Wotan, *meinem Eide! —*
die biet' ich mit mir zum Bund.

HAGEN.

(hinter ihnen stehend.)

Doch des Niblungenhortes
nennt die Märe dich Herrn?

SIEGFRIED.

Des Schatzes vergaß ich fast, —
so schätz' ich sein müß'ges Gut!
In einer Höhle ließ ich's liegen,
wo ein Wurm einst es bewacht.

HAGEN.

Und nichts entnahmst du ihm?

SIEGFRIED.

(auf ein metallenes Gewirk deutend, das er am Gürtel trägt.)

Dieß Gewirk, unkund seiner Kraft.

HAGEN.

Die Tarnkappe *kenn' ich,*
*der Niblungen kunst*reiches *Werk;*
sie taugt, bedeckt sie *dein Haupt,*
dir zu tauschen jede Gestalt;
verlangst du an fernsten Ort,
sie entführt flugs dich dahin. —
Sonst nichts entnahmst du dem Hort?

GUNTHER

> Happily greet, o hero,
> The hall of my father:
> Wherever you go
> Whatever you see —
> Consider that your own.
> Yours is my heritage,
> Land and people —
> Support my oath, Wotan! —
> I give myself as your vassal.

SIEGFRIED

> I offer no land or people,
> Nor a father's house or court:
> His only legacy
> The right to vengeance —
> That I have used up alone.
> I have only my weapons
> — I won them myself —
> Support my oath, Wotan! —
> I offer them, and myself, as your ally.

HAGEN

(standing behind them)

> But the Niblung hoard,
> Rumor says you are its lord?

SIEGFRIED

> I almost forgot the treasure —
> So lightly I value its idle possession!
> I left it lying in a cave,
> Where a dragon once watched over it.

HAGEN

> And you took nothing from it?

SIEGFRIED

(pointing to a metal chain mail, which he carries on his belt)

> This chain mail, I don't know its powers.

HAGEN

> I recognize the Tarnkappe,
> The skillful work of the Niblungs:
> It can, if it covers your head,
> Change you into any shape;
> If you wish to be far away,
> It will take you there instantly. —
> Did you take nothing else from the hoard?

SIEGFRIED.
>   *Einen Ring.*

HAGEN.
>   *Den hütest du wohl?*

SIEGFRIED.
>   *Ihn hütet ein hehres Weib.*

HAGEN.
(für sich.)
>   *Brünnhild!*

GUNTHER.
>   *Nicht, Siegfried, sollst du mir tauschen!*
>   *Tand gäb' ich für dein Geschmeid',*
>   *nähmst all' mein Gut du dafür:*
>   *ohn' Entgelt dien' ich dir gern.*

(Hagen ist zu Gudrune's Thür gegangen und öffnet sie jetzt. Gudrune tritt heraus; sie trägt ein gefülltes Trinkhorn und naht damit Siegfried.)

GUDRUNE.
>   *Willkommen, Gast, in Gibich's* Halle!
>   *Seine Tochter reicht dir den Trank.*

SIEGFRIED.
(neigt sich ihr freundlich und ergreift das Horn; er hält es gedankenvoll vor sich hin und sagt leise.)
>   *Vergäß' ich alles was du gabst,*
>   *von einer Lehre lass' ich nie:*
>   *den ersten Trunk zu treuer Minne,*
>   *Brünnhilde,* trink' *ich dir!*

(Er trinkt und reicht das Horn Gudrunen zurück, welche, in großer Verschämtheit, verwirrt ihr Auge vor ihm niederschlägt.)

SIEGFRIED.
(den Blick in Theilnahme auf sie heftend.)
>   *Was senkst du so den Blick?*

GUDRUNE.
(schlägt erröthend das Auge zu ihm auf.)

SIEGFRIED.
>   *Gunther, wie heißt deine Schwester?*

GUNTHER.
>   *Gudrune.*

SIEGFRIED
    A ring.
HAGEN
    You keep it safe?
SIEGFRIED
    A noble woman keeps it safe.
HAGEN
(to himself)
    Brünnhild!
GUNTHER
    Siegfried, you should exchange nothing with me!
    I could give only baubles for your jewels,
    Even if you took all of my possessions for it:
    I will serve you gladly without payment

(Hagen has gone to Gudrune's door and now opens it. Gudrune comes out; she carries a filled drinking horn and approaches Siegfried with it.)

GUDRUNE
    Welcome, guest, in Gibich's hall!
    His daughter now offers you drink.
SIEGFRIED
(bows in a friendly manner to her and takes the horn. He holds it thoughtfully before him and says quietly.)
    If I were to forget all that you gave me
    I shall never forsake one lesson:
    The first drink of true love,
    Brünnhilde, I drink to you!

(He drinks and gives the horn back to Gudrune,
who, greatly embarrassed, sinks her eyes in confusion before him.)

SIEGFRIED
(gazing with interest at her)
    Why do you sink your gaze?
GUDRUNE
(blushing, raises her eyes to him)
SIEGFRIED
    Gunther, what is your sister's name?
GUNTHER
    Gudrune

SIEGFRIED.

Wohl *gute Runen*
läßt mich ihr Auge lesen.

(Er faßt sie sanft bei ihrer Hand.)

Deinem Bruder bot ich mich zum Manne, —
der Stolze schlug mich aus:
Trügst du, wie er, mir Übermuth,
bot' ich mich dir zum Bund?

GUDRUNE.
(neigt demüthig das Haupt, und mit einer Gebärde, als sei sie nicht seiner
werth, verläßt sie wankenden Schrittes wieder die Halle.)

SIEGFRIED.
(blickt ihr wie festgezaubert nach, von Hagen und Gunther aufmerksam
beobachtet; — dann, ohne sich zu wenden, fragt er.)

Hast du, Gunther, ein Weib?

GUNTHER.

Nicht freit' ich noch, und einer Frau
soll ich mich schwerlich freuen:
auf Eine setzt' ich den Sinn,
die kaum ich erringen soll.

SIEGFRIED.
(lebhaft sich zu ihm wendend.)

Was sollte versagt dir sein,
steht meine Stärke dir bei?

GUNTHER.

Auf Felsen hoch ihr Sitz,
ein Feuer umbrennt den Saal:
nur, wer durch das Feuer bricht,
darf Brünnhilde's Freier sein

SIEGFRIED.

Nicht fürchte ihr Feuer,
ich freie sie für dich.
Denn dein Mann bin ich,
und mein Muth ist dein,
erwerb' *ich Gudrun zum Weib.*

GUNTHER.

Gudrune gönn' ich dir gern.

SIEGFRIED.

Brünnhilde bringe ich dir.

GUNTHER.

Wie willst du sie täuschen?

SIEGFRIED

Certainly they are good runes
Her eyes bid me read.

(He takes her gently by the hand.)

I offered myself to your brother as vassal —
The proud man refused me:
Would you, like him, be so proud,
If I were to offer myself to you?

GUDRUNE

(bows her head modestly, and making a gesture as if she were unworthy of
him, she leaves the hall with unsteady gait.)

SIEGFRIED

(gazes after her entranced, watched closely by Hagen and Gunther — then,
without turning, he asks.)

Do you, Gunther, have a wife?

GUNTHER

I have not yet sought one, and a wife
I shall probably never enjoy:
I have set my heart on one
That I can scarcely win.

SIEGFRIED

(quickly turning to him)

What should be refused to you,
If I support you with my strength?

GUNTHER

Her seat is on a high rock,
A fire surrounds her hall;
Only the one who can break through the fire
Can be Brünnhilde's wooer.

SIEGFRIED

Do not fear her fire,
I'll woo her for you.
For I am your vassal,
And my courage is yours,
If I win Gudrun as wife.

GUNTHER

I'll grant Gudrun to you gladly.

SIEGFRIED

I'll bring Brünnhilde to you.

GUNTHER

How can you deceive her?

SIEGFRIED.
>*Durch des Tarnhelms Trug*
>*tausch' ich mir deine Gestalt.*
GUNTHER.
>*So stelle Eide zum Schwur.*
SIEGFRIED.
>*Blutbrüderschaft* schließe *der Eid!*

(Hagen füllt ein Trinkhorn mit frischem Wein. Siegfried und Gunther ritzen sich mit ihren Schwertern die Arme und halten diese eine kurze Weile über das Trinkhorn.)

SIEGFRIED und GUNTHER.
>Wotan, weihe den Trank,
>Treue zu trinken dem Freund!
>Waltender, wahre den Eid
>heilig einiger Brüder! —
>Dem Blut entblühe der Bund,
>dem gebrochen — Rächer du seist! —
>Bricht ihn ein Bruder,
>trügend den Treuen,
>treffe dein Zorn
>zehrend den Zagen,
>fliege dein Fluch
>dem Fliehenden nach,
>schleud're dem Schlund
>Hellja's ihn hin!
>Wotan, weihe den Trank!
>Waltender, wahre den Eid!

(Sie trinken nach einander, jeder zur Hälfte; dann zerschlägt Hagen, welcher während des Schwures bei Seite gelehnt, das Horn; Siegfried und Gunther reichen sich die Hände.)

SIEGFRIED.
(zu Hagen.)
>*Was nahmst du am Eid nicht Theil?*
HAGEN.
>*Mein Blut verdürb' euch den Trank;*
>*nicht fließt mir's ächt und edel wie euch,*
>*störrisch und kalt stockt's in mir,*
>*nicht will's die Wangen mir röthen:*
>*drum bleib' ich fern vom feurigen Bund.*

SIEGFRIED
>   Through the Tarnhelm's deception
>   I will exchange my shape with yours.

GUNTHER
>   Let us then swear an oath.

SIEGFRIED
>   Let blood-brotherhood seal the oath!

(Hagen fills the drinking horn with fresh wine. Siegfried and Gunther nick their arms with their swords and hold them briefly over the horn.)

SIEGFRIED and GUNTHER
>   Wotan, consecrate the drink,
>   To drink fealty to my friend!
>   Ruler god, keep the oath
>   Holy between brothers! —
>   Let the bond between us spring from the blood,
>   A bond which, if broken, you will avenge.
>   If a brother breaks it
>   Betraying the true one,
>   Let your anger fall
>   Consuming the coward;
>   Let your curse fly
>   After the one who flees,
>   Let him be thrown
>   Into the jaws of Hell!
>   Wotan, consecrate the drink,
>   Ruler god, protect the oath!

(They drink, one after the other, each one half: then Hagen, who has been standing aside, shatters the horn; Siegfried and Gunther grasp one another's hands.)

SIEGFRIED
(to Hagen)
>   Why did you not take part in the oath?

HAGEN
>   My blood would have spoiled the drink:
>   It does not flow noble and pure like yours,
>   Stagnant and cold it stands in my veins,
>   It won't even redden my cheeks:
>   So I avoid the fiery bond.

GUNTHER.

Laß den unfrohen Mann!

SIEGFRIED.

Frisch auf die Fahrt! Dort liegt mein Schiff,
schnell bringt es zu Brünnhild's Felsen;
eine Nacht am Ufer harrst du mein,
die Frau dann führ' ich dir zu.

GUNTHER.

Rastest du nicht zuvor?

SIEGFRIED.

Um die Rückkehr ist's mir jach.

(Er geht zum Ufer.)

GUNTHER.

Nun, *Hagen, bewache die Halle!*

(Er folgt Siegfried.)
(Gudrune erscheint an der Thüre ihres Gemaches.)

GUDRUNE.

Wohin eilen die Schnellen?

HAGEN.

Zu Schiff, Brünnhilde zu freien.

GUDRUNE.

Siegfried?

HAGEN.

Sieh', wie's ihn treibt
zum Weib dich zu erwerben.

(Er setzt sich mit Speer und Schild vor der Halle nieder. Siegfried und Gunther fahren ab.)

GUDRUNE.

Siegfried — mein!

(Sie geht lebhaft erregt in ihr Gemach zurück.)
(Ein Teppich schlägt vor der Scene zusammen und verschließt die Bühne. — Nachdem der Schauplatz verwandelt ist, wird der Teppich gänzlich aufgezogen.)

GUNTHER
>Leave the unhappy man alone!

SIEGFRIED
>Quickly on our way! There lies my boat,
>It will bring us quickly to Brünnhilde's rock;
>You will wait for me one night on the shore,
>Then I will lead the woman to you.

GUNTHER
>Won't you rest first?

SIEGFRIED
>I am eager for the return.

(He goes to the bank.)

GUNTHER
>Now, Hagen, keep watch over the hall!

(He follows Siegfried.)
(Gudrune appears at the door of her chamber.)

GUDRUNE
>Where are the bold ones going?

HAGEN
>To the boat. To win Brünnhilde.

GUDRUNE
>Siegfried?

HAGEN
>Look how he is driven
>To win you as wife.

(He sits down with his spear and shield before the hall. Siegfried and Gunther depart.)

GUDRUNE
>Siegfried — mine!

(She goes eagerly back into her chamber.)
(A tapestry closes before the scene and hides the stage. —
After the scene has been changed, the tapestry is raised
completely out of the way.)

Dritte Scene.

(Die Felsenhöhle wie im Vorspiele. — Brünnhilde sitzt am Eingange des
Steingemaches, in tiefes Sinnen versunken. Von rechts her vernimmt man,
anfangs wie aus weiter Ferne, dann allmählich immer näher kommend, Gesang
der Walküren. Nach dem ersten Rufe der Walküren fährt Brünnhilde auf und
lauscht aufmerksam.)

DIE WALKÜREN.
    Brünnhild! Brünnhild! Verlor'ne Schwester! —
    Verloschen das Feuer um den Felsensaal!
    Wer hat es bewältigt! Wer hat dich erweckt?
BRÜNNHILDE.
    Euch grüß' ich, ferne Schwestern!
    Forscht ihr nach der Verlor'nen?
    Wohl ist erloschen das Feuer,
    seit er es bewältigt, der mich erweckt:
    Siegfried, der herrliche Held.
DIE WALKÜREN.
    Brünnhild! Brünnhild! Nun bist du sein Weib!
    Das Roß nicht wirst du mehr reiten,
    nicht mehr dich schwingen zur Schlacht.
BRÜNNHILDE.
    So zürnte es Wotan der Unverzagten,
    die Siegfried's Vater schützte im Kampf
    gegen des Gottes Geheiß:
    denn friedlos war er auf Frikka's Wort,
    weil Ehe er brach, um den ächtesten Sohn
    mit der eig'nen Schwester zu zeugen.
DIE WALKÜREN.
    Brünnhild! Brünnhild! Verlor'ne Schwester!
    Wer lehrte dich trotzen dem Lenker der Schlacht?
BRÜNNHILDE.
    Die leuchtenden Wälsungen lehrt' er mich immer
    zu schützen in drängender Schlacht;
    nicht wollt' ich für Siegmund weichen:
    beschildet von mir schon zückt' er das Schwert
    auf Hunding, der Schwester Gemahl;
    doch an Wotan's Speer zersprang die Waffe,
    die der Gott einst selbst ihm gegeben: —
    hin sank er im Streit, — bestraft ward ich.

Third Scene

(The rocky cave as in the prelude. — Brünnhilde sits at the entrance of
the stone chamber, lost in deep thought. From the right one can hear, first as
if from a great distance, then gradually getting closer, the song of the
Valkyries. After the first call of the Valkyries Brünnhilde starts and listens
carefully.)

THE VALKYRIES
    Brünnhild! Brünnhild! Lost sister! —
    The fire has gone out around your rocky hall!
    Who conquered it? Who awakened you?
BRÜNNHILDE
    I greet you, distant sisters!
    Are you searching for the lost one?
    The fire has truly gone out,
    Since he conquered it, the one who awakened me
    Siegfried, the magnificent hero.
THE VALKYRIES
    Brünnhild! Brünnhild! Now you are his wife!
    You will no longer ride the steed,
    No longer ride into battle.
BRÜNNHILDE
    So angry was Wotan about the fearless one,
    Who protected Siegfried's father in battle
    Against the god's command:
    For he was outlawed by Frikka's command,
    For committing adultery, in order to conceive
    The purest son with his own sister.
THE VALKYRIES
    Brünnhild! Brünnhild! Lost sister! —
    Who taught you to disobey the ruler of battles?
BRÜNNHILDE
    He taught me to protect the glorious Volsungs
    Always in violent battle;
    I didn't wish to give in for Siegmund:
    Protected by me, he drew his sword
    Against Hunding, the sister's husband;
    But the weapon shattered on Wotan's spear,
    The weapon the god himself had once given him:
    He fell then in battle: I was punished.

DIE WALKÜREN.

Brünnhild! Brünnhild!
Nun ward'st du geschieden aus der Wunschmädchen Schaar,
auf den Felsen gebannt, in Schlaf versenkt,
bestimmt dem Manne zum Weib,
der am Weg dich fänd' und erweckt'!

BRÜNNHILDE.

Daß der Muthigste nur mich gewänne,
gewährte mir Wotan den Wunsch,
daß wildes Feuer den Felsen umbrenne:
nur Siegfried, wußt' ich, würd' es durchschreiten.

DIE WALKÜREN.

(immer näher kommend, während die Bühne sich immer mehr verfinstert.)
Brünnhild! Brünnhild! Verlor'ne Schwester!
Gab'st du nun hin deine hehre Kraft?

BRÜNNHILDE.

Ich weihte sie Siegfried, der mich gewann.

DIE WALKÜREN.

Gab'st du nun hin dein heiliges Wissen,
die Runen, die Wotan dich lehrte?

BRÜNNHILDE.

Ich lehrte sie Siegfried, den ich liebe.

DIE WALKÜREN.

Dein Roß, das treu über Wolken dich trug?

BRÜNNHILDE.

Das zäumt nun Siegfried, da in Streit er zog.

DIE WALKÜREN.

(immer näher.)
Brünnhild! Brünnhild! Verlor'ne Schwester!
Jeder Zage kann dich nun zwingen,
dem Feigsten bist du zur Beute! —
O brennte das Feuer neu um den Felsen,
vor Schande die schwache Genossin zu schützen!
Wotan! Waltender! Wende die Schmach!

(Finstere Gewitterwolken ziehen immer dichter am Himmel auf und senken
sich auf den Saum der Felsenhöhe.)

BRÜNNHILDE.

So weilet, ihr Schwestern! Weilet, ihr Lieben!
Wie stürmt mir das Herz euch Starke zu seh'n!
O weilet! O laßt die Verlor'ne nicht!

THE VALKYRIES
> Brünnhild! Brünnhild!
> Now you have been cast out from the wish-maidens' band,
> Exiled to this rock, bound in sleep,
> Fated to become wife to the man
> Who would find you along the way and awaken you.

BRÜNNHILDE
> So that only the most courageous could win me,
> Wotan granted my wish
> That wild fire burn around this rock,
> Only Siegfried, I knew, would come through it.

THE VALKYRIES
(coming ever closer, as the stage gradually gets darker)
> Brünnhild! Brünnhild! Lost sister! —
> Have you given up your glorious power?

BRÜNNHILDE
> I dedicated it to Siegfried, who won me.

THE VALKYRIES
> Did you give him your holy knowledge,
> The runes, which Wotan taught you?

BRÜNNHILDE
> I taught them to Siegfried, whom I love.

THE VALKYRIES
> Your steed, that faithfully carried you through the clouds?

BRÜNNHILDE
> He is now bridled by Siegfried, because he rode him to battle.

THE VALKYRIES
(ever closer)
> Brünnhild! Brünnhild! Lost sister! —
> Any coward can now control you,
> You are booty for the most craven!
> If only the fire still burned around the rock,
> To protect the weakened comrade from shame.
> Wotan! Ruling god! Turn away this dishonor.

(Dark storm clouds collect in the heavens and sink onto the edge of the rocky cave.)

BRÜNNHILDE
> So remain here sisters! Remain, dear ones!
> How my heart rejoices at seeing you, the strong ones!
> O remain! Don't leave the lost one behind!

DIE WALKÜREN.
(in nächster Nähe, während von daher, wo sie kommen, ein blendender Glanz
durch die schwarzen Wolken bricht.)

    Nach Süden wir ziehen, Siege zu zeugen,
    kämpfenden Heeren zu kiesen das Loos,
    für Helden zu fechten, Helden zu fällen,
    nach Walhall zu führen erschlagene Sieger!

(Die Walküren, acht an der Zahl, ziehen in strahlender Waffenrüstung und auf
weißen Roßen reitend, in dem Glanze über dem schwarzen Wolkensaum mit
stürmischem Geräusch vorüber. — Am Saume der Felsenhöhe bricht ringsum
ein dichtes Feuer aus.)

BRÜNNHILDE.
(in heiliger Ergriffenheit.)

    Wotan! Wotan!
    Zorngnädiger Gott!
    Den herrlichsten Helden zu lieben
    lehrte dein Strafen mich:
    der traulich in Walhall
    das Trinkhorn oft du entnahmst,
    sie willst du der Schmach nicht weih'n.
    Des Feuers heiliger Bote
    entbietet mir froh deine Huld:
    der Kraft und des Wissens ledig,
    deines Grußes leb' ich noch werth!
    Es brennt das Feuer um Brünnhilde's Fels!
    Dank Wotan! Waltender Gott!

(Siegfried's Hornruf läßt sich aus der Tiefe vernehmen; Brünnhilde lauscht, —
ihre Züge verklären sich in höchster Freude.)

    Siegfried! Siegfried ist nah'!
    Seinen Gruß *sendet er her!* —
    Verglimme, machtlose Gluth!
    Ich steh' in stärk'rem Schutz!

(Sie eilt freudig dem Hintergrunde zu.)

THE VALKYRIES
(Very close to her, while from the direction they are coming a bright light
breaks through the dark clouds.)

> We are going to the south, to produce victories,
> To choose the fate of battling armies,
> To fight for heroes, to fell them as well,
> To lead the fallen victors to Valhalla.

(The Valkyries, eight in number, pass over the black clouds in their shining
armor and on white steeds with the sound of thunder and lightning. — At the
edge of the rocky cave a dense fire breaks out.)

BRÜNNHILDE
(in holy emotion)

> Wotan! Wotan!
> O god, compassionate in your anger!
> Your punishment taught me
> To love the greatest of heroes.
> The one from whom you often
> Received the drinking horn in Valhalla,
> You will not deliver her to shame.
> The fire is your holy messenger
> Bringing me your protection:
> Having lost power and knowledge,
> I am still worthy of your greeting!
> The fire burns now around Brünnhilde's rock!
> Thanks be to Wotan! The ruling god!

(Siegfried's horn call can be heard in the distance; Brünnhilde listens — her
features are transfigured by the greatest joy.)

> Siegfried! Siegfried is near!
> He sends his greetings to me! —
> Die away, powerless fire!
> I stand in stronger protection.

(She hurries joyfully toward the background.)

Vierte Scene.

(Siegfried, den Tarnhelm auf dem Haupte, der ihm zur Hälfte das Gesicht deckt und nur die Augen frei läßt, erscheint in Gunther's Gestalt, indem er aus dem Feuer heraus auf einen emporragenden Felsstein springt. — Das Feuer brennt sogleich matter und erlischt bald ganz.)

BRÜNNHILDE.
(voll Entsetzen zurückweichend.)
　　Verrath! *Verrath! Wer drang zu mir?*

(Sie flieht bis in den Vordergrund und heftet von da aus in sprachlosem Erstaunen ihren Blick auf Siegfried.)

SIEGFRIED.
(im Hintergrunde auf dem Steine verweilend, betrachtet sie lange auf seinen Schild gelehnt; dann redet er sie mit verstellter [tieferer] Stimme langsam und feierlich an.)
　　Bist du Brünnhild, die muthige Maid,
　　die weithin die Helden schreckt
　　durch ihr trotziges Herz?
　　Zitternd weichst du mir fern,
　　fliehst dem Hündlein gleich,
　　das des Herrn Züchtigung fürchtet?
　　Der freisliche Zauber zehrenden Feuers
　　war dir wahrlich Gewinn,
　　denn er schützte das schwächste Weib!
BRÜNNHILDE.
(dumpf vor sich hin.)
　　Das schwächste Weib!
SIEGFRIED.
　　Brannte der Muth dir nur,
　　so lange das Feuer brannte?
　　Sieh', es verlischt, und der Waffen ledig
　　zwing' ich dich Weib durch dein zages Herz.
BRÜNNHILDE.
(zitternd.)
　　Wer ist der Mann, der das vermochte,
　　was dem Stärksten nur bestimmt?

Fourth Scene

(Siegfried, the Tarnhelm on his head, which hides half of his face and only leaves his eyes free, appears in Gunther's shape, as he springs out of the fire onto a jutting rock. — The fire burns less fiercely and soon goes out entirely.)

BRÜNNHILDE
(shocked, pulling back)
    Betrayal! Betrayal! Who has forced his way to me?

(She flees into the foreground and fastens her gaze from there in speechless astonishment on Siegfried.)

SIEGFRIED
(In the background lingering on the rock, gazes at her for a long time leaning on his shield; then he speaks with a disguised [deeper] voice slowly and solemnly to her.)
    Are you Brünnhild, the courageous maiden
    Who frightens the heroes far and wide
    Through her stubborn heart?
    Trembling you shrink away from me,
    You flee like a little dog
    That fears its master's punishment?
    The fearful magic of the destructive flames
    Was a great gain for you,
    For it protected the weakest of women!
BRÜNNHILDE
(dully to herself)
    The weakest of women!
SIEGFRIED
    Did your courage only burn
    As long as the fire burned?
    Look, it went out, and lacking weapons
    I conquer you, woman, through your fearful heart.
BRÜNNHILDE
(trembling)
    Who is the man who could accomplish
    What was only allowed to the strongest?

SIEGFRIED.

(immer noch auf dem Steine im Hintergrunde.)

> Der vielen Helden Einer,
> die härt're Gefahr bestanden,
> als hier ich finde bestimmt.
> Büßen sollst du mir bald,
> daß durch bange Märe die Männer du schreckest,
> als brächt' es Verderben, um Brünnhild zu frei'n.
> Doch aller Welt will ich nun zeigen,
> wie zahm daheim in der Halle ein Weib
> mir züchtig spinnt und webt.

BRÜNNHILDE.

> *Wer bist du?*

SIEGFRIED.

> Ein Bess'rer als der,
> den du zum Gatten verdienst.
> *Ein Gibichung bin ich,*
> *und Gunther heißt der Held,*
> *dem, Frau, du folgen sollst.*

BRÜNNHILDE.

(in Verzweiflung ausbrechend.)

> *Wotan, ergrimmter, grausamer Gott!*
> *Weh', nun erseh' ich der Strafe Sinn:*
> *Zu Hohn und Jammer jagst du mich hin!*

(Sich ermannend.)

> Doch hört' ich ein Horn — Siegfried's Horn?

SIEGFRIED.

> Der heit're Held hütet das Schiff,
> darin du morgen mir folgest:
> wohl übt er munt're Weisen.

BRÜNNHILDE.

> Siegfried? — Du lügst!

SIEGFRIED.

> Er wies mir den Weg.

BRÜNNHILDE.

> Nein! — Nein!

SIEGFRIED.

(näher tretend.)

> *Die Nacht bricht an:*
> *in deinem Gemach*
> *mußt du dich mir vermählen.*

SIEGFRIED
(still on the rock in the background)
>One of the many heroes
>Who have stood up to worse dangers
>Than those I find here.
>You shall soon atone
>For frightening men with wild stories,
>That it would bring ruin to woo Brünnhild.
>But I will now show all the world
>How tamely a woman
>Spins and weaves for me in my hall.

BRÜNNHILDE
>Who are you?

SIEGFRIED
>A better man than the one
>You deserve as a husband.
>I am a Gibichung
>And the hero is named Gunther,
>Whom, woman, you shall follow.

BRÜNNHILDE
(breaking out in desperation)
>Wotan, angry, cruel god!
>Woe, now I see the sense of the punishment:
>You drive me to mockery and misery!

(taking control of herself)
>But I heard a horn — Siegfried's horn?

SIEGFRIED
>The merry hero guards the boat,
>In which you will accompany me tomorrow:
>He is probably practicing merry melodies.

BRÜNNHILDE
>Siegfried? — You are lying!

SIEGFRIED
>He showed me the way.

BRÜNNHILDE
>No! — No!

SIEGFRIED
(coming closer)
>Night is falling:
>In your chamber
>You must be wed to me.

BRÜNNHILDE.
(den Finger, an dem sie Siegfried's Ring trägt, drohend emporstreckend.)
> *Bleib' fern! Fürchte dieß Zeichen!*
> *Zur Schande zwingst du mich nicht,*
> *so lang' der Ring mich schützt.*

SIEGFRIED.
> *Mannesrecht geb' er Gunther:*
> *durch den Ring sei ihm vermählt!*

BRÜNNHILDE.
> *Zurück, Räuber!*
> *Frevelnder Dieb,*
> *erfreche nicht dich zu nahen!*
> *Stärker* wie *Stahl*
> *macht mich der Ring,*
> *nie — raubst du ihn mir.*

SIEGFRIED.
> *Von dir ihn zu lösen lehrst du mich nun.*

(Er dringt auf sie ein: sie ringen. Brünnhilde windet sich los und flieht. Siegfried setzt ihr nach, — sie ringen von Neuem: er faßt sie und entzieht ihrem Finger den Ring. Sie schreit laut auf und sinkt wie zerbrochen auf den Stein vor dem Gemach zusammen.)

SIEGFRIED.
> *Jetzt bist du mein!*
> *Brünnhilde, Gunther's Braut,*
> *gönne mir nun dein Gemach!*

BRÜNNHILDE.
(fast ohnmächtig.)
> *Was könntest du wehren, elendes Weib?*

(Siegfried treibt sie mit einer gebietenden Gebärde an: zitternd geht sie mit wankenden Schritten in das Gemach voran.)

SIEGFRIED.
(sein Schwert ziehend.)
> Nun, Balmung, bewahre du
> dem Bruder meine Treu'!

(Er folgt ihr nach.)

Der Vorhang fällt.

BRÜNNHILDE
(threateningly holding up the finger on which she wears Siegfried's ring)
> Keep away! Fear this sign!
> You cannot force me to shame,
> As long as this ring protects me.

SIEGFRIED
> Let it give Gunther a husband's right:
> Be wed to him with this ring!

BRÜNNHILDE
> Back, robber!
> Felonious thief,
> Do not dare to come near me!
> The ring makes me
> Stronger than steel,
> Never — can you tear it from me.

SIEGFRIED
> You have shown me that I must take it from you.

(He closes on her: they struggle. Brünnhilde escapes and flees. Siegfried pursues her — they struggle again: he holds her and forces the ring from her finger. She cries out and sinks as if broken onto the rocks in front of the chamber.)

SIEGFRIED
> Now you are mine!
> Brünnhilde, Gunther's bride,
> Grant me now your chamber!

BRÜNNHILDE
(almost senseless)
> How can you defend yourself, miserable woman?

(Siegfried drives her forward with a commanding gesture: trembling she goes with uncertain steps ahead of him into the chamber.)

SIEGFRIED
(drawing his sword)
> Now, Balmung, protect
> My fidelity to my brother!

(He follows her.)

The curtain falls

Zweiter Akt.

(Uferraum vor der Halle der Gibichungen: rechts der offene Eingang zur Halle, links das Rheinufer, von dem aus sich eine felsige Anhöhe quer über die Bühne nach rechts zu erhebt. — Es ist Nacht.)

Erste Scene.

(Hagen, den Speer im Arm, den Schild zur Seite, sitzt schlafend an der Halle. Der Mond wirft plötzlich ein grelles Licht auf ihn und seine nächste Umgebung: man gewahrt Alberich, den Nibelung, vor Hagen, die Arme auf dessen Kniee gelehnt.)

ALBERICH.
    Schläfst du, Hagen, mein Sohn? —
    Du schläfst und hörst mich nicht,
    den ruhlos Kummerreichen?
HAGEN.
(leise und ohne sich zu rühren, so daß er noch fort zu schlafen scheint.)
    Ich höre dich, schlimmer Albe;
    was kommst du mir *zu sagen?*
ALBERICH.
    Wissen sollst du,
    welche Macht du hast —
    bist du so stark und *muthig*
    wie deine *Mutter dich gebar.*
HAGEN.
(immer wie zuvor.)
    Gab sie mir Muth und Stärke,
    nicht doch mag ich ihr danken,
    daß deiner List sie erlag:
    früh alt, bleich und fahl,
    hass' ich die Frohen,
    freue mich nie.
ALBERICH.
    Hagen, mein Sohn, nicht hasse mich,
    denn Großes geb' ich in deine Hand.
    Der Ring, nach dem ich zu ringen dich lehrte,
    wisse nun, was er verschließt.
    Dem Tod und der Nacht in Nibelheim's Tiefe

Second Act

(River bank area before the hall of the Gibichungs: on the right the open entrance to the hall, to the left, the bank of the Rhine, from which a rocky height rises across the stage to the right. — It is night.)

First Scene

(Hagen, his spear in his arm, his shield at his side, sits asleep in the hall. The moon suddenly throws a harsh light on him and his surroundings: Alberich, the Nibelung, can now be seen in front of Hagen, resting his arms on the latter's knees.)

ALBERICH
    Are you asleep, Hagen, my son? —
    You sleep and do not hear me,
    The restless sufferer?
HAGEN
(softly and without moving, so that he still seems to sleep)
    I hear you, evil elf:
    What have you come to say to me?
ALBERICH
    You should know,
    What power you have —
    If you are strong and courageous
    Just as your mother bore you.
HAGEN
(always as before)
    If she gave me courage and strength
    I still cannot thank her
    That she gave in to your cunning:
    Old too soon, pale and sallow,
    I hate the joyous,
    I am never happy.
ALBERICH
    Hagen, my son, do not hate me,
    For I place into your hand great power.
    The ring, for which I taught you to fight,
    Know now, what it contains.
    From the death and darkness in Nibelheim's depth

entkeimten die Nibelungen;
kunstreiche Schmiede, rastlos schaffend,
regen die Erde sie auf.
Das Rheingold entwandt' ich der Wassertiefe,
schuf aus ihm einen Ring:
durch seines Zaubers zwingende Kraft
zähmt' ich das fleißige Volk;
ihrem Herrn gehorchend, hieß ich sie schaffen;
den eig'nen Bruder hielt ich in Banden:
den Tarnhelm mußte Mime mir schmieden,
durch ihn bewahrt' ich wachsam mein Reich.
Den gewalt'gen Hort häufte ich so,
der sollte die Welt mir gewinnen.
Da regt' ich Sorge den Riesen auf,
die Plumpen plagte der Neid;
den jungen Göttern boten sie Gunst,
eine Burg ihnen bauten die Dummen,
von der sie nun herrschen in sich'rer Hut:
doch den Hort bedangen die Riesen zum Dank. —
Hörst du, Hagen, mein Sohn?

HAGEN.

Die Götter? . . .

ALBERICH.

Mit listiger Fessel fingen sie mich,
zur Lösung ließ ich den Hort;
einzig wahren wollt' ich den Ring,
doch ihn auch raubten sie mir:
da verflucht' ich ihn, in fernster Zeit
zu zeugen den Tod dem, der ihn trüg'.
Selbst wollte Wotan ihn wahren,
doch es trotzten die Riesen: auf der Nornen Rath
wich Wotan
vor eig'nem Verderben gewarnt.
Machtlos müht' ich mich nun,
mich band der Ring, wie die Brüder er band;
unfrei sind wir nun alle.
Rastlos und rührend rüsten wir nichts:
sank auch der Riesen trotzige Sippe
längst vor der Götter leuchtendem Glanz,
ein träger Wurm, den als Wächter sie zeugten,
hielt doch gefesselt unsre Freiheit:
den Ring! den Ring! den Ring! —
Schläfst du, Hagen, mein Sohn?

Arose the Nibelungs:
Artistic smiths, restlessly toiling,
They animate the earth.
I stole the Rheingold from the depths of the water,
Made from it a ring:
Through its magical controlling power
I tamed the industrious folk:
Obedient to their lord, I bade them work;
I held my own brother in bonds:
Mime had to forge the Tarnhelm for me,
With it, I was able to keep watch on my kingdom.
The mighty hoard I piled up so;
It was supposed to gain me the world.
Then I aroused the concern of the giants,
The clumsy ones were plagued by envy;
They courted the young gods' favor,
The stupid ones built them a castle,
From which they now safely reign:
But the giants demanded the hoard in exchange. —
Do you hear, Hagen, my son?

HAGEN

The gods? . . .

ALBERICH

With cunning fetters they captured me.
As ransom I paid with the hoard;
I wished to keep only the ring,
But they stole even it from me:
I cursed it, in that distant time
To bring death to any who wore it.
Wotan wanted to keep it himself,
But the giants demanded it: advised by the Norns
Wotan gave in
Warned of his own ruin.
Powerless I struggled,
The ring bound me, as it bound my brothers;
We are now all unfree.
Restless and stirring we accomplish nothing:
Even though the stubborn race of the giants
Has sunk before the bright fame of the gods,
A lazy dragon, which they conceived as guard,
Kept our freedom fettered;
The ring! The ring! The ring! —
Are you asleep, Hagen, my son?

HAGEN.

    Doch nun erschlug Siegfried den Wurm?

ALBERICH.

    Mime der Falsche führte den Helden,
    den Hort durch ihn zu gewinnen:
    der weise Thor! Daß dem Wälsung er traute,
    sein Leben ließ er drum.
    Götterentspross'nen traut' ich nie,
    sie erbten treulose Art:
    dich Unverzagten zeugt' ich mir selbst,
    du, Hagen, hältst mir Treu'!
    Doch wie stark du bist,
    nicht ließ ich den Wurm dich besteh'n:
    nur Siegfried mochte das wagen, —
    verderben sollst du nun Den.
    Thor auch er!
    Tand dünkt ihn der Ring,
    dessen Macht er nicht erräth.
    Mit List und Gewalt entreiß' ihm den Ring!
    Mit List und Gewalt raubten die Götter ihn mir.

HAGEN.

    Den Ring sollst du haben.

ALBERICH.

    Schwörst du es mir?

HAGEN.

    Niblungenfürst, frei sollst du sein!

(Ein immer finsterer Schatten bedeckt wieder Hagen und Alberich. Vom Rheine her dämmert der Tag.)

ALBERICH.

(wie er allmählich immer mehr dem Blicke entschwindet, wird auch seine Stimme immer unvernehmbarer.)

    Sei treu, Hagen, mein Sohn!
    Trauter Helde, sei treu!
    Sei treu! — Treu!

(Alberich ist gänzlich verschwunden. Hagen, der unverrückt in seiner Stellung verblieben, regt sich nicht und blickt starren Auges nach dem Rheine hin. — Die Sonne geht auf und spiegelt sich in der Fluth.)

HAGEN

But now Siegfried has slain the dragon?

ALBERICH

Mime, the false one, led the hero,
Hoping to gain the hoard through him:
The wise fool! Since he trusted the Volsung,
He lost his life for that.
I never trusted the descendents of gods,
They have inherited treacherous character:
I myself conceived you, O fearless one,
You, Hagen, will keep faith with me!
Even though you are strong,
I did not have you challenge the dragon:
Only Siegfried could dare that task ——
You shall now destroy him.
He is also a fool!
He thinks the ring a trinket,
Whose power he never guessed.
With cunning and strength tear the ring from him!
With cunning and strength the gods stole it from me.

HAGEN

You shall have the ring.

ALBERICH

Do you swear it to me?

HAGEN

Prince of Nibelungs, you shall be free!

(An ever darkening shadow again covers Hagen and Alberich. The day begins
to break over the Rhine.)

ALBERICH

(As he gradually disappears from view, his voice becomes more and more
inaudible.)

Be true, Hagen, my son!
Trusted hero, be true.
Be true! — True!

(Alberich has disappeared completely. Hagen, who has remained motionless
throughout, does not move but stares with fixed gaze toward the Rhine. —
The sun rises and is mirrored in the water.)

Zweite Scene.

(Siegfried tritt plötzlich dicht am Ufer hinter einem Busche hervor: er ist in
seiner eigenen Gestalt, nur die Tarnkappe hat er noch auf dem Haupte; er
zieht sie ab und hängt sie in den Gürtel.)

SIEGFRIED.
> *Hoiho! Hagen,* wacht *müder Mann!*
> *Siehst du mich kommen!*

HAGEN.
(langsam sich erhebend.)
> *Hei! Siegfried, geschwinder Helde!*
> *Wo brausest du her?*

SIEGFRIED.
> *Vom Brünnhildenstein;*
> *dort sog ich den Athem ein,*
> *mit dem ich* jetzt *dich rief:*
> *so* rasch *war meine Fahrt!*
> *Langsamer folgt mir ein Paar,*
> *zu Schiff gelangt das her.*

HAGEN.
> *So zwangst du Brünnhilde?*

SIEGFRIED.
> *Wacht Gudrune schon?*

HAGEN.
(laut rufend.)
> *Hoiho! Gudrun! Komm' heraus!*
> *Siegfried ist da,* der rasche Recke.

SIEGFRIED.
(zur Halle sich wendend.)
> *Euch beiden meld' ich, wie ich Brünnhild band.*

(Gudrune tritt ihnen unter der Halle entgegen.)

SIEGFRIED.
> *Heiß' mich willkommen, Gibichskind!*
> *Ein guter Bote bin ich dir.*

GUDRUNE.
> *Freija grüße dich*
> *zu aller* Jungfrau'n *Ehre!*

SIEGFRIED.
> Freija, die Holde, heiß' ich dich:
> Frikka laß uns nun rufen,

Second Scene

(Siegfried appears suddenly from behind a bush close to the bank. He is in his own shape, but he still has the Tarnkappe on his head; he removes it and hangs it on his belt.)

SIEGFRIED
    Hoiho! Hagen, weary watchman!
    Do you see me coming?
HAGEN
(rising slowly)
    Hey! Siegfried, fleet hero
    Where are you rushing from?
SIEGFRIED
    From Brünnhilde's rock;
    There I drew in the breath,
    With which I just called you.
    That's how fast my journey was!
    A couple is following me more slowly,
    They are coming by boat.
HAGEN
    So you conquered Brünnhilde?
SIEGFRIED
    Is Gudrune already awake?
HAGEN
(calling loudly)
    Hoiho! Gudrun! Come out!
    Siegfried is here, the swift warrior.
SIEGFRIED
(turning toward the hall)
    I will tell you both how I bound Brünnhilde.

(Gudrune approaches them from below the hall.)

SIEGFRIED
    Welcome me, child of Gibich!
    I am a good messenger to you.
GUDRUNE
    May Freija greet you
    In honor of all maidens!
SIEGFRIED
    I call you Freija, the dear one:
    Let us now call Frikka,

Wotan's heilige Gattin,
sie gönne uns gute Ehe!

GUDRUNE.

So folgt Brünnhild meinem Bruder?

SIEGFRIED.

Leicht ward die Frau ihm gefreit.

GUDRUNE.

Sengte das Feuer ihn nicht?

SIEGFRIED.

Ihn hätt' es nicht versehrt;
*doch ich durch*drang *es für ihn,*
da dich ich wollt' erwerben.

GUDRUNE.

Und dich hatt' es verschont?

SIEGFRIED.

Es schwand um mich und erlosch.

GUDRUNE.

Hielt Brünnhild dich für Gunther?

SIEGFRIED.

Ihm glich ich auf ein Haar;
Der Tarnhelm wirkte das,
wie Hagen mich es wies.

HAGEN.

Dir gab ich guten Rath.

GUDRUNE.

So zwangst du das kühne Weib?

SIEGFRIED.

Sie wich — Gunther's Kraft.

GUDRUNE.

Und vermählte sie sich dir?

SIEGFRIED.

Ihrem Mann gehorchte Brünnhild
eine volle bräutliche Nacht.

GUDRUNE.

Als ihr Mann doch galtest du?

SIEGFRIED.

Bei Gudrun weilte Siegfried.

GUDRUNE.

Doch zur Seite war ihm Brünnhild?

SIEGFRIED.

(auf sein Schwert deutend.)

Zwischen Ost und West — der Nord:
so nah' — war Brünnhild ihm fern.

Wotan's holy spouse,
Let her grant us good marriage!

GUDRUNE

So Brünnhilde is following my brother?

SIEGFRIED

The woman was easily won for him.

GUDRUNE

Didn't the fire burn him?

SIEGFRIED

It would not have harmed him;
But I went through it for him,
Since I wanted to win you.

GUDRUNE

And it spared you?

SIEGFRIED

It disappeared around me and went out.

GUDRUNE

Did Brünnhilde think you were Gunther?

SIEGFRIED

I matched every hair on his head;
The Tarnhelm accomplished that,
Just as Hagen had told me.

HAGEN

I gave you good advice.

GUDRUNE

So you conquered the bold woman?

SIEGFRIED

She gave in — to Gunther's strength.

GUDRUNE

And was wed to you?

SIEGFRIED

Brünnhilde obeyed her husband
A whole bridal night.

GUDRUNE

But you posed as her husband?

SIEGFRIED

Siegfried was with Gudrun.

GUDRUNE

But Brünnhilde was at your side?

SIEGFRIED

(pointing to his sword)

Between East and West — the North:
So near — Brünnhilde was far away.

GUDRUNE.
Wie empfing sie nun Gunther von dir?
SIEGFRIED.
Im Frühnebel vom Felsen
folgte sie mir hinab;
dem Strande nah' — flugs die Stelle
tauschte Gunther mit mir;
durch des Geschmeides Tugend
wünscht' ich mich schnell hierher.
Ein starker Wind nun treibt
die Trauten den Rhein herauf:
drum rüstet nun *den Empfang!*
GUDRUNE.
Siegfried, allmächt'ger *Mann!*
Wie fürcht' ich mich vor dir!
HAGEN.
(von der Anhöhe im Hintergrunde den Rhein hinabspähend.)
In der Ferne seh' ich ein Segel.
SIEGFRIED.
So sagt dem Boten Dank!
GUDRUNE.
Laßt sie uns hold empfangen,
daß heiter und gern sie weile!
Du, Hagen, rufe die Mannen
zur Hochzeit an Gibich's Hof!
Ich rufe Frauen zum Fest,
der Freudigen folgen sie gern.

(Zu Siegfried, nach der Halle voran schreitend.)

Willst du nicht rasten, *schlimmer Held?*
SIEGFRIED.
Dir zu helfen ruh' ich aus.

(Er folgt ihr. Beide gehen in die Halle ab.)

GUDRUNE

How did Gunther receive her from you?

SIEGFRIED

She followed me down from the rock

In early morning fog;

Near to the beach — quickly I changed

Places with Gunther.

The power of the Tarnhelm

Brought me instantly here.

A strong wind now drives

The dear ones up the Rhine:

Now we must prepare to receive them.

GUDRUNE

Siegfried, almighty man!

How I am afraid of you!

HAGEN

(from the high ground in the background looking down the Rhine)

I see a sail in the distance.

SIEGFRIED

So give the messenger your thanks!

GUDRUNE

Let her greet us joyfully.

So that she will remain happy here!

You, Hagen, call together the men

To the wedding at Gibich's court!

I'll call the women to the festival,

They will happily follow me, the joyful one.

(To Siegfried, striding toward the hall.)

Won't you rest, terrible hero?

SIEGFRIED

I'll rest by helping you.

(He follows her. Both go off into the hall.)

Dritte Scene.

HAGEN.
(auf der Anhöhe stehend, stößt, der Landseite zugewandt, mit aller Kraft in ein großes Stierhorn.)
Hoiho! Hoiho! Hoiho!
Ihr Gibich's Mannen, machet euch auf!
Wehe! Wehe! Waffen durch's Land!
Waffen! Waffen! Gute Waffen!
Starke Waffen! Scharf zum Streit!
Noth! Noth ist da! Noth! Wehe! Wehe!
Hoiho! Hoiho! Hoiho!

(Er bläst abermals: vom Lande her antworten aus verschiedenen Richtungen Heerhörner. Von den Höhen und aus der Ebene stürzen in heftiger Eile gewaffnete Mannen herbei.)

DIE MANNEN.
(erst einzelne, dann mehrere.)
Was tos't das Horn? Was ruft es zu Heer?
Wir kommen zur Wehr, wir kommen mit Waffen!
Mit starken Waffen, *mit scharfer Wehr!*
Hoiho! Hoiho! Hagen! Hagen!
Welche Noth ist da? Welcher Feind ist nah'?
Wer giebt uns Streit? Ist Gunther in Noth?
HAGEN.
(von der Anhöhe herab.)
Rüstet euch wohl und rastet nicht!
Gunther sollt ihr empfangen,
ein Weib hat der gefreit.
DIE MANNEN.
Drohet ihm Noth? Drängt ihn der Feind?
HAGEN.
Ein freisliches Weib führet er heim.
DIE MANNEN.
Ihm folgen der Magen feindliche Mannen?
HAGEN.
Einsam fährt er, mit ihr allein.
DIE MANNEN.
So bestand er die Noth, bestand den Kampf?
HAGEN.
Der Wurmtödter wehrte der Noth,
Siegfried, der Held, der schuf ihm Heil.

Third Scene

HAGEN
(standing on the high rock and facing the land, he blows with all his might a large steerhorn.)

> Hoiho! Hoiho! Hoiho!
> Gibich's Vassals, arise!
> Woe! Woe! With weapons through the land!
> Weapons! Weapons! Good weapons!
> Strong weapons! Sharp for the battle!
> Danger, Danger is here! Danger! Woe! Woe!
> Hoiho! Hoiho! Hoiho!

(He blows the horn again, other horns answer him from various directions. Armed men rush in from the heights and the plains.)

THE VASSALS
(first individually, then together)

> Why does the horn sound? Why are we called to battle?
> We come for defense, we come with weapons!
> With strong weapons, with sharp swords!
> Hoiho! Hoiho! Hagen! Hagen!
> What kind of danger is there? Which enemy is near?
> Who offers us battle? Is Gunther in danger?

HAGEN
(from the high rock)

> Arm yourselves and do not rest!
> You must welcome Gunther,
> He has won a wife.

THE VASSALS

> Is he in danger? Is the enemy in pursuit?

HAGEN

> He brings home a terrifying woman.

THE VASSALS

> Her hostile relatives are pursuing him?

HAGEN

> He brings her home alone.

THE VASSALS

> So he withstood the battle, withstood the danger?

HAGEN

> The dragon-slayer held off the danger,
> Siegfried, the hero, protected him there.

DIE MANNEN.

> *Was soll das Heer nun noch helfen?*

HAGEN.

> *Starke Stiere sollt ihr schlachten,*
> *am Weihstein fließe Wotan ihr Blut!*

DIE MANNEN.

> Was dann, Hagen? Was sollen wir dann?

HAGEN.

> *Einen Eber fällen sollt ihr für Froh,*
> *einen stämmigen Bock stechen für Donner;*
> *Schafe aber schlachtet für Frikka,*
> *daß gute Ehe sie gebe!*

DIE MANNEN.

(in immer mehr ausbrechender Heiterkeit.)

> *Schlugen wir Thiere, was schaffen wir dann?*

HAGEN.

> *Das Trinkhorn nehmt von trauten Frauen,*
> *mit Meth und Wein wonnig gefüllt.*

DIE MANNEN.

> Tranken wir aus, was treiben wir dann?

HAGEN.

> Trinken so lang, bis im Rausch ihr lallt,
> *Alles den Göttern zu Ehren,*
> *daß gute Ehe sie geben!*

DIE MANNEN.

(in schallendes Lachen ausbrechend.)

> *Groß Glück und Heil lacht nun dem Rhein,*
> da der grimme Hagen *so lustig mag sein!*
> *Der Hagedorn sticht nun nicht mehr,*
> *zum Hochzeitrufer ward er bestellt.*

HAGEN.

(der immer sehr ernst geblieben.)

> *Nun laßt das Lachen,*
> *muthige Mannen!*
> *Empfangt Gunther's Braut,*
> *Brünnhild naht dort mit ihm.*

(Er ist herabgestiegen.)

> *Hold seid der Herrin, helfet ihr treu:*
> *traf sie ein Leid — rasch seid zur Rache!*

THE VASSALS
> What should the army do to help now?

HAGEN
> You should slay strong steers
> So that their blood flows on the altar to Wotan.

THE VASSALS
> What then, Hagen? What should we do then?

HAGEN
> You should kill a boar for Froh,
> Stab a brawny ram for Donner;
> Sacrifice sheep for Frikka,
> So she will bestow a good marriage.

THE VASSALS
(in rising merriment)
> When we have sacrificed the beasts, what then?

HAGEN
> Take the drinking horn from dear women,
> Filled with mead and wine.

THE VASSALS
> When we have emptied the horns, what then?

HAGEN
> Drink so long until you drunkenly stammer
> Everything to the honor of the gods,
> So they will bestow a good marriage!

THE VASSALS
(breaking out in pealing laughter)
> Great luck and joy laughs now on the Rhine,
> Since the grim Hagen can be so merry!
> The hawthorn no longer pricks,
> He now plays the wedding herald.

HAGEN
(who has remained very serious.)
> Stop your laughing
> Courageous vassals!
> Receive Gunther's bride,
> Brünnhild approaches with him.

(He has descended from the rock.)

> Be dear to the lady, help her truly:
> If any harm has come to her — be quick to revenge!

Vierte Scene.

(Gunther ist mit Brünnhilde im Nachen angekommen. Einige springen in das Wasser und ziehen den Kahn zum Strand; während Gunther Brünnhilde an das Land geleitet, schlagen die Mannen jauchzend an die Waffen. Hagen steht zur Seite im Hintergrunde.)

DIE MANNEN.
> *Heil! Heil! Heil! Heil!*
> *Willkommen! Willkommen!*
> Heil dir, *Gunther!*
> Heil deiner Braut!

GUNTHER.
(Brünnhilde an der Hand führend.)
> *Brünnhild, die* herrlichste *Frau,*
> *bring' ich euch her zum Rhein;*
> *ein edleres Weib ward nie gewonnen!*
> *Der Gibichungen Geschlecht,*
> *gaben die Götter ihm Gunst,*
> *zu höchstem Ruhm rag' es nun auf!*

DIE MANNEN.
(an die Waffen schlagend.)
> *Heil! Heil dir,* Gunther!
> *Glücklicher Gibichung!*

(Brünnhilde, bleich und mit zu Boden gesenktem Blicke, folgt Gunther, der sie an der Hand zur Halle geleitet, aus welcher jetzt Siegfried und Gudrune an der Spitze von Frauen heraustreten.)

GUNTHER.
(mit Brünnhilde vor der Halle anhaltend.)
> *Gegrüßt sei, theurer Helde!*
> *Gegrüßt sei, holde Schwester!*
> *Dich seh' ich froh zur Seite*
> ihm, der zur Frau dich erkor.
> *Zwei selige Paare seht hier prangen:*
> *Brünnhilde und Gunther,*
> *Gudrune und Siegfried!*

BRÜNNHILDE.
(erschrickt, schlägt die Augen auf und erblickt Siegfried: sie läßt Gunther's Hand fahren, geht heftig bewegt einen Schritt auf Siegfried zu, weicht entsetzt zurück und heftet starr den Blick auf ihn. — Alle sind sehr betroffen.)

Fourth Scene

(Gunther has arrived with Brünnhilde in the boat. Several men spring into the water and pull it onto the shore. While Gunther leads Brünnhilde onto the land, the vassals strike their weapons together in joy. Hagen stands aside in the background.)

THE VASSALS
    Hail! Hail! Hail! Hail!
    Welcome! Welcome!
    Hail to you, Gunther!
    Hail to your bride!
GUNTHER
(leading Brünnhilde by the hand)
    Brünnhilde, the most magnificent woman,
    I bring to you here on the Rhine;
    A more noble woman has never been won!
    The gods have given their favor
    To the race of the Gibichungs,
    It will now rise to its highest fame.
THE VASSALS
(striking their weapons together)
    Hail, Hail to you Gunther!
    Fortunate Gibichung!

(Brünnhilde, pale and with her eyes turned to the ground, follows Gunther, who now leads her to the hall from which Siegfried and Gudrune at the head of the women's train now emerge.)

GUNTHER
(stopping before the hall with Brünnhilde)
    Greetings to you, dear hero!
    Greetings to you, beloved sister!
    I see the one who has chosen you as wife
    Joyfully standing at your side.
    Two blessed pairs I see here in their glory:
    Brünnhilde and Gunther,
    Gudrune and Siegfried!
BRÜNNHILDE
(startled, raises her eyes and sees Siegfried: she drops Gunther's hand, goes in great agitation a a step toward Siegfried, steps back in shock and stares at him. — Everyone is deeply affected.)

DIE MANNEN und FRAUEN.
Was ist ihr?
SIEGFRIED.
(geht ruhig einige Schritte auf Brünnhilde zu.)
Welche Sorge mach' ich dir, Brünnhild?
BRÜNNHILDE.
(kaum ihrer mächtig.)
Siegfried ... hier! ... Gudrune? ...
SIEGFRIED.
Gunther's milde Schwester,
mir vermählt, wie Gunther du.
BRÜNNHILDE.
Wie? ... Gunther? ... Du lügst! —
Mir schwindet das Licht ...

(Sie droht umzusinken; Siegfried, ihr zunächst stehend,
stützt sie.)

BRÜNNHILDE.
(matt und leise in Siegfried's Arm.)
Siegfried ... kennt mich nicht?
SIEGFRIED.
Gunther, deinem Weib ist übel.

(Gunther tritt hinzu.)

Erwache, Frau! — Hier ist dein Gatte.

(Indem Siegfried mit dem Finger auf Gunther deutet, erblickt Brünnhilde an
ihm den Ring.)

BRÜNNHILDE.
(im heftigsten Schreck.)
Ha! Der Ring — an seiner Hand —!
Er — Siegfried —!
DIE MANNEN und FRAUEN.
Was ist?
HAGEN.
(aus dem Hintergrunde unter die Mannen tretend.)
Merket wohl, was die Frau euch klagt!
BRÜNNHILDE.
(sie ermannt sich, die furchtbarste Aufregung gewaltsam zurückhaltend.)
Einen Ring sah ich an deiner Hand, —
nicht dir gehört er, ihn entriß mir —

THE VASSALS and WOMEN
    What's the matter with her?
SIEGFRIED
(quietly goes a few steps toward Brünnhilde.)
    What distress do I cause you, Brünnhilde?
BRÜNNHILDE
(scarcely able to contain herself)
    Siegfried . . . here . . . Gudrune? . . .
SIEGFRIED
    Gunther's sweet sister,
    Wed to me as you to Gunther.
BRÜNNHILDE
    How? . . . Gunther? . . . You are lying!
    I am fainting . . .

(She threatens to collapse; Siegfried, who is standing closest to her, supports her.)

BRÜNNHILDE
(weak and softly on Siegfried's arm)
    Siegfried . . . doesn't know me?
SIEGFRIED
    Gunther, your wife is ill.

(Gunther steps closer.)

    Awaken lady — here is your husband.

(When Siegfried points to Gunther with his finger, Brünnhilde sees the ring on it.)

BRÜNNHILDE
(deeply shocked)
    Ha! The ring — on his hand — !
    He — Siegfried — !
THE VASSALS and WOMEN
    What is it?
HAGEN
(from the background, emerging from among the vassals)
    Pay close attention to this woman's accusation!
BRÜNNHILDE
(She regains control over herself, holding back the most powerful agitation.)
    I saw a ring on your hand —
    It does not belong to you, it was torn from me —

(auf Gunther deutend.)

> *dieser Mann: —*
> *Wie mochtest von ihm den Ring du empfah'n?*

SIEGFRIED.

(betrachtet aufmerksam den Ring an seiner Hand.)

> *Den Ring empfing ich — nicht von ihm.*

BRÜNNHILDE.

(zu Gunther.)

> *Nahmst du von mir den Ring,*
> *durch den ich dir vermählt,*
> *so melde ihm dein Recht,*
> *ford're zurück das Pfand!*

GUNTHER.

(in großer Verwirrung.)

> *Den Ring? — Ich gab ihm keinen. —*
> *Doch — kennst du ihn auch gut?*

BRÜNNHILDE.

> *Wo bärgest du den Ring,*
> *den du von mir erbeutet?*

GUNTHER.

(schweigt in höchster Betroffenheit.)

BRÜNNHILDE.

(wüthend auffahrend.)

> *Ha! — Dieser war's,*
> *der mir den Ring entriß, —*
> *Siegfried, der trugvolle Räuber!*

SIEGFRIED.

(der über den Ring in sinnendes Schweigen entrückt war.)

> *Von keinem Weib bekam ich ihn,*
> *noch war's ein Weib,*
> *dem ich ihn abgewann.*
> *Genau erkenn' ich des Kampfes Lohn,*
> *den auf Neidhaide einst ich bestand,*
> *als den starken Wurm ich erschlug.*

HAGEN.

(zwischen sie tretend.)

> *Brünnhild, kühne Frau,*
> *kennst du genau den Ring?*
> *Ist's der, den Gunther du gabst,*
> *so ist er sein, —*
> *und Siegfried gewann ihn durch Trug,*
> *den der Treulose büßen sollt'!*

(pointing to Gunther)
>by this man —
>How could you have received the ring from him?

SIEGFRIED
(looks carefully at the ring on his hand.)
>I did not get the ring — from him.

BRÜNNHILDE
(to Gunther)
>If you took the ring from me
>With which you were wed to me,
>So make your rightful claim,
>Demand back your pledge.

GUNTHER
(greatly confused)
>The ring? — I gave him none. —
>But — do you recognize it for certain?

BRÜNNHILDE
>Where did you put the ring
>That you stole from me?

GUNTHER
(stands in astonished silence)

BRÜNNHILDE
(exploding in anger)
>Ha! — It was this one,
>Who took the ring from me —
>Siegfried, the treacherous robber!

SIEGFRIED
(who has been lost in thought looking at the ring)
>I received this ring from no woman,
>Nor was it a woman
>From whom I won it.
>I recognize perfectly battle's reward,
>Which I won on Neidhaide,
>As I killed the strong dragon.

HAGEN
(stepping between them)
>Brünnhild, bold woman,
>Do you recognize the ring with certainty?
>If it is the one you gave Gunther,
>Then it is his —
>And Siegfried gained it through deceit.
>Which the faithless one should pay for!

BRÜNNHILDE.
(im furchtbarsten Schmerze aufschreiend.)
> *Betrug! Betrug!*
> *O schändlichster Betrug!*
> *Verrath! Verrath,*
> *wie er noch nie gerächt!*

GUDRUNE. DIE MANNEN und FRAUEN.
> *Verrath! Betrug! An wem?*

BRÜNNHILDE.
> *Heil'ge Götter! Himmlische Lenker!*
> *Rauntet ihr dieß in eurem Rath?*
> *Lehrt ihr mich Leiden, wie Keiner sie litt?*
> *Schuft ihr mir Schmach, wie nie sie geschmerzt?*
> *Rathet nun Rache, wie nie sie geras't!*
> *Zündet mir Zorn, wie nie er gezähmt!*
> *Zeiget Brünnhild, wie ihr Herz* sie zerbreche —
> *den zu* vernichten, *der sie* verrieth!

GUNTHER.
> *Brünnhild, Gemahlin! Mäß'ge dich!*

BRÜNNHILDE.
> *Weich' fern, Betrüger, selbst* betrog'ner! —
> *Wisset denn Alle: nicht — ihm,*
> *dem Mann dort bin ich vermählt.*

DIE MANNEN und FRAUEN.
> *Siegfried? Gudrun's Gemahl?*

BRÜNNHILDE.
> *Er zwang mir Lust und Liebe ab.*

SIEGFRIED.
> *Achtest du so der eig'nen Ehre?*
> *Die Zunge, die sie lästert,*
> *muß ich der Lüge sie zeih'n?*
> *Hört, ob ich Treue brach!*
> *Blutbrüderschaft*
> *hab' ich und Gunther geschworen:*
> Balmung, mein *werthes Schwert,*
> *wahrte der Treue Eid;*
> *mich trennte seine Schärfe*
> *von diesem traurigen Weib!*

BRÜNNHILDE.
> *Du listiger Held, sieh', wie du lügst,*
> *wie auf dein Schwert du schlecht dich berufst!*
> *Wohl kenn' ich die Schärfe, doch kenn' auch die Scheide,*
> *darin so wonnig ruht' an der Wand*

BRÜNNHILDE
(crying out in greatest pain)
> Deceit! Deceit!
> O most shameless deceit!
> Betrayal! Betrayal,
> As has never been avenged!

GUDRUNE, THE VASSALS, and WOMEN
> Betrayal, Deceit. Of whom?

BRÜNNHILDE
> Holy gods, heavenly rulers!
> Did you decide this in your council?
> Are you teaching me to suffer as no one ever suffered?
> Have you made shame for me, more painful than any?
> Now teach me vengeance, as it has never raged!
> Set me afire in anger, that can never be tamed!
> Show Brünnhilde how she can break her heart —
> To destroy the one who betrayed her!

GUNTHER
> Brünnhild, my wife! Calm yourself!

BRÜNNHILDE
> Get away from me, betrayer, betrayed yourself! —
> All of you shall know: Not — to him
> But to him there I am married.

THE VASSALS and WOMEN
> Siegfried? Gudrun's husband?

BRÜNNHILDE
> He forced pleasure and love from me.

SIEGFRIED
> Do you value your own honor so little?
> The tongue that abuses it
> Must I now accuse of lying?
> Hear whether I broke my oath!
> Blood-brotherhood
> I swore with Gunther:
> Balmung, my mighty sword,
> Protected the oath of fidelity;
> Its sharp blade separated me
> From this unhappy woman!

BRÜNNHILDE
> You cunning hero, look how you lie!
> How you basely call on your sword!
> I know well its sharp blade, but I also know its sheath,
> In which it remained on the wall.

Balmung, *der treue Freund,*
als die Traute sein Herr sich gefreit.

DIE MANNEN.

(in lebhafter Entrüstung zusammentretend.)

    Wie? Brach er die Treue?
    Trübte er Gunther's Ehre?

GUNTHER.

    Geschändet wär' ich, schmählich bewahrt,
    gäbst du die Rede nicht ihr zurück!

GUDRUNE.

    Treulos, Siegfried, solltest du sein?
    Bezeuge, daß falsch jene dich zeiht!

DIE MANNEN.

    Reinige dich, bist du im Recht.
    Schweige die Klage, schwöre den Eid!

SIEGFRIED.

    Schweig' ich die Klage, schwör' ich den Eid, —
    wer von euch wagt seine Waffe daran?

HAGEN.

    Meines Speeres Spitze wag' ich daran,
    Wotan möge sie weih'n!

(Die Mannen schließen einen Ring um Siegfried; Hagen hält ihm die Spitze seines Speeres hin; Siegfried legt zwei Finger seiner rechten Hand darauf.)

SIEGFRIED.

    Wotan! Wotan! Wotan!
    Hilf meinem heiligen Eide!
    Hilf durch die wuchtende Waffe,
    hilf durch des Speeres Spitze!
    Wo mich Scharfes schneidet,
    schneide sie mich,
    wo der Tod mich trifft,
    treffe sie *mich:*
    klagte das Weib dort wahr,
    brach ich dem Bruder die Treu'!

BRÜNNHILDE.

(tritt wüthend in den Ring, reißt Siegfried's Hand vom Speer, und faßt dafür mit der ihrigen die Spitze.)

    Höre mich, herrliche Göttin!
    Hüterin heiliger Eide!
    Hilf durch die wuchtende Waffe,
    hilf durch des Speeres Spitze!

Balmung, the faithful friend,
As its master wed his beloved.

THE VASSALS
(coming together in great shock)
How? Did he break faith?
Did he darken Gunther's honor?

GUNTHER
I would be dishonored, held in shame,
If you don't refute her accusation.

GUDRUNE
Siegfried, you are accused of being faithless?
Prove that that woman accuses you falsely.

THE VASSALS
Exonerate yourself, if you are in the right.
Silence the accusation, swear the oath!

SIEGFRIED
If I silence the accusation, if I swear the oath —
Who will dare extend his weapon for it?

HAGEN
My spearpoint I will dare to offer.
Let Wotan bless it.

(The vassals close a ring around Siegfried; Hagen extends the point of his spear; Siegfried lays two fingers of his right hand on it.)

SIEGFRIED
Wotan! Wotan! Wotan!
Aid my holy oath!
Aid through the weighty weapon,
Aid through the spear's point!
Wherever a sharp edge can cut me,
Let it cut me
Where death can strike me,
Let it strike me:
If that woman accuses aright;
If I broke faith with my brother!

BRÜNNHILDE
(strides angrily into the ring, tears Siegfried's hand from the spear, and takes hold of the point it with her own.)
Hear me, magnificent goddess!
Protector of holy oaths!
Aid through the weighty weapon,
Aid through the spear's point!

Weih' ihre Wucht,
daß ihn sie werfe,
segne die Schärfe,
daß ihn sie schneide:
denn brach seine Eide er all',
schwur Meineid jetzt dieser Mann!
DIE MANNEN.
(in höchstem Aufruhr.)
Hilf Donner! Tose dein Wetter,
zu schweigen die wüthende Schmach!
SIEGFRIED.
Gunther! Wehr' deinem Weibe,
das schamlos Schande dir lügt! —
Gönnt ihr Weil' und Ruh',
der wilden Felsenfrau,
daß die freche Wuth sich lege,
die eines Unhold's List
durch bösen Zauber's Trug
wider uns aufgeregt. —
Ihr Mannen, kehret euch ab,
laßt das Weibergekeif'!
Auf, kommt für den Weihstein
weidliche Stiere zu schmücken:
folget in's Weihgeheg',
für Froh den Eber zu fangen. —

(Zu den Frauen.)

Auch ihr helfet zur Hochzeit,
folget Gudrunen, ihr Frauen!

(Er geht mit Gudrune in die Halle, die Mannen und Frauen folgen ihnen.)

Hallow its weight,
That it can be thrown against him,
Bless the sharpness,
So that it can cut him:
For as he broke all of his oaths,
This man has now committed perjury!

THE VASSALS
(in great agitation)
Help, Donner! Let your storm rage,
To silence this raging dishonor!

SIEGFRIED
Gunther! Control your wife,
Who shamelessly sullies you with lies! —
Grant her time and rest,
The wild woman of the cliffs,
So that her insolent rage can subside,
Which a demon's cunning
Through the trickery of evil magic
Has brought up against us. —
You vassals, turn away
Leave women's squabbling behind!
Come, let us decorate steers
For the sacrificial altar:
Follow me to the holy grove,
To catch a boar for Froh. —

(To the women.)

You also must help prepare the wedding,
Follow Gudrun, all of you women.

(He goes with Gudrune into the hall. The vassals and women follow him.)

Fünfte Scene.

(Brünnhilde, Gunther und Hagen bleiben zurück. — Gunther hat sich in
tiefer Scham und furchtbarer Verstimmung, mit verhülltem Gesichte abseits
niedergesetzt.)

BRÜNNHILDE.
(im Vordergrunde stehend und vor sich hin starrend.)
> *Welches Unhold's List liegt hier* verborgen?
> *Welches Zauber's Rath regte dieß auf?*
> *Wo ist nun mein Wissen gegen dieß Wirrsal,*
> *wo sind meine Runen gegen dieß Räthsel?*
> *Ach, Jammer, Jammer! Weh'! Ach! Weh'!*
> *All' mein Wissen wies ich ihm zu!*
> *In seiner Macht hält er die Magd,*
> *in seinen Banden faßt er die Beute,*
> *die, jammernd ob ihrer Schmach, —*
> *jauchzend der Reiche verschenkt!*
> *Wer bietet mir nun das Schwert,*
> *mit dem ich die Bande zerschnitt'?*

HAGEN.
(dicht an sie herantretend.)
> *Vertraut mir, betrog'ne Frau!*
> *Wer dich verrieth, das räche ich.*

BRÜNNHILDE.
> *An wem?*

HAGEN.
> *An Siegfried, der dich betrog.*

BRÜNNHILDE.
> *An Siegfried? — Du?*

(Sie lacht bitter.)

> *Ein einz'ger Blick seines* glänzenden *Auges,*
> *das selbst durch die Lügengestalt*
> *leuchtend strahlte zu mir, —*
> *deinen besten Muth* schlüg' er zu Boden!

HAGEN.
> *Wohl kenn' ich Siegfried's siegende Kraft,*
> *wie schwer im Kampf er zu fällen:*
> *drum raune mir nun* klugen *Rath,*
> *wie mir der Recke wohl wich'?*

Fifth Scene

(Brünnhilde, Gunther, and Hagen remain behind. — Gunther sits off to the side in deep shame and frightful agitation with his face turned away and covered.)

BRÜNNHILDE
(standing in the foreground, staring straight ahead)
>   What demon's cunning lies hidden here?
>   What sort of magic aroused this?
>   Where is my wisdom against this confusion,
>   Where are my runes against this puzzle?
>   Oh, Misery, Misery, Woe, Oh, Woe!
>   I have given him all of my wisdom!
>   He holds the maiden in his power,
>   He binds the captured one in his bonds,
>   Whom, whimpering in her shame,
>   The rich one joyously gives away!
>   Who offers me now the sword
>   With which I can cut these bonds?

HAGEN
(steps close to her)
>   Trust me, betrayed woman!
>   Whoever betrayed you, I will avenge you.

BRÜNNHILDE
>   On whom?

HAGEN
>   On Siegfried, who betrayed you.

BRÜNNHILDE
>   On Siegfried? — you?

(She laughs bitterly.)

>   A single glance of his burning eye,
>   Which even through the lying shape
>   Shot its rays to me —
>   He would strike down your best courage!

HAGEN
>   I know well Siegfried's victorious strength,
>   How difficult he would be to fell in battle:
>   Thus you must give me wise advice,
>   How the warrior would fall to me?

BRÜNNHILDE.

> *O, Undank! Schändlicher Lohn!*
> *Nicht eine Kunst war mir bekannt,*
> *die zum Heil nicht half seinem* kühnen *Leib!*
> *Unwissend zähmt' ihn mein Zauberspiel,*
> *das ihn vor Wunden nun gewahrt.*

HAGEN.

> *So kann keine* Waffe *ihm schaden?*

BRÜNNHILDE.

> *Im Kampfe nicht! — doch: —*
> *Träfest du im Rücken ihn,*
> *niemals, das wußt' ich, wich' er dem Feind,*
> *nie reicht' er ihm fliehend den Rücken,*
> *an ihm drum spart' ich den Segen.*

HAGEN.

> *Und dort trifft ihn mein Speer.*

(Sich rasch zu Gunther wendend.)

> *Auf, Gunther! Edler Gibichung!*
> *Hier steht dein starkes Weib, —*
> *was hängst du dort in Harm?*

GUNTHER.

(auffahrend.)

> *O Schmach! O Schande. Wehe mir,*
> *dem jammervollsten Manne!*

HAGEN.

> *In Schande liegst du, läugn' ich das?*

BRÜNNHILDE.

> *O feiger Mann! Falscher Genoß!*
> *Hinter dem Helden hehltest du dich,*
> *Preise des Ruhms dir zu erringen.*
> *Tief wohl sank das theure Geschlecht,*
> *das solche Zagen erzeugt*

GUNTHER.

(außer sich.)

> *Betrüger ich — und betrogen!*
> *Verräther ich — und verrathen!*
> *Zermalmt mir das Mark,*
> *zerbrecht mir die Brust!*
> *Hilf, Hagen! Hilf meiner Ehr'!*
> *Hilf deiner Mutter,*
> *die mich auch gebar!*

BRÜNNHILDE

O, ingratitude, shameful repayment!
Not a single skill was known to me
That did not help to protect his bold body!
My magic tamed him unaware;
It now protects him from wounds.

HAGEN

So no weapon can harm him?

BRÜNNHILDE

Not in battle! But:
If you struck him in the back,
Never — that I knew — would he give way to an enemy,
Never would he turn his back in flight,
Therefore I spared my spells there.

HAGEN

And there my spear will strike him.

(Turning quickly to Gunther.)

Arise, Gunther! Noble Gibichung!
Here stands your strong wife —
Why are you sitting there in grief?

GUNTHER

(startled)

O shame, O dishonor. Woe is me,
The most miserable of men.

HAGEN

You lie in shame, do I deny that?

BRÜNNHILDE

O coward! False comrade!
You hid behind the hero,
To gain the prize of fame for you.
The race that produced such cowards
Has truly sunk low!

GUNTHER

(beside himself)

I am the swindler — and the one swindled!
I am the betrayer — and also the one betrayed!
Crush my marrow
Break open my breast!
Help, Hagen! Help my honor!
Help your mother,
Who also bore me!

HAGEN.

Dir hilft kein Hirn, dir hilft keine Hand:
dir hilft nur Siegfried's Tod!

GUNTHER.

Siegfried's — Tod!

HAGEN.

Nur der sühnt deine Schmach.

GUNTHER.

(von Grausen gepackt vor sich hin starrend.)
Blutbrüderschaft schwuren wir uns!

HAGEN.

Des Bundes Bruch sühne nun Blut!

GUNTHER.

Brach er den Bund?

HAGEN.

Da er dich verrieth.

GUNTHER.

Verrieth er mich?

BRÜNNHILDE.

Dich verrieth er, —
und mich verriethet ihr alle!
Wär' ich gerecht, alles Blut der Welt
büßte mir nicht eure Schuld!
Doch des Einen Tod taugt mir für Alle,
Siegfried — falle
zur Sühne für sich und euch!

HAGEN.

(nahe zu Gunther gewendet.)
Er falle dir zum Heile!
Ungeheure Macht wird dir,
gewinnst du von ihm den Ring,
den der Tod ihm nur entreißt.

GUNTHER.

Brünnhilde's Ring!

HAGEN.

Den Ring der Nibelungen.

GUNTHER.

— So wär' es Siegfried's Ende!

HAGEN.

Uns Allen frommt sein Tod.

HAGEN

    No brain can help you; no hand can help you:

    You can only be helped by Siegfried's death.

GUNTHER

    Siegfried's — death!

HAGEN

    Only that can redeem your honor.

GUNTHER

(shaken with horror, staring straight ahead)

    We swore blood-brotherhood!

HAGEN

    Let the breaking of the bond be paid with blood.

GUNTHER

    Did he break the bond?

HAGEN

    When he betrayed you.

GUNTHER

    Did he betray me?

BRÜNNHILDE

    He betrayed you —

    And you have all betrayed me!

    If I were just, all the blood in the world

    Would not repay your guilt!

    But the death of the one will stand for all,

    Let Siegfried fall

    As atonement for himself and for you!

HAGEN

(turning close to Gunther)

    Let him fall to your advantage!

    You will gain great power

    If you win the ring from him,

    Which can only be taken from him by death.

GUNTHER

    Brünnhilde's ring!

HAGEN

    The Ring of the Nibelungs.

GUNTHER

    — Then it would be Siegfried's end!

HAGEN

    His death will profit us all.

GUNTHER.

> *Doch Gudrun, ach, der ich ihn gönnte!*
> *Straften den Gatten wir so,*
> *wie bestünden wir vor ihr?*

BRÜNNHILDE.

(wild auffahrend.)

> *Was rieth mir mein Wissen? Was wiesen mich Runen?*
> *Im hilflosen Elend* seh' ich hell:
> *Gudrune heißt der Zauber,*
> *der mir den Gatten entzückt.*
> *Angst treffe sie!*

HAGEN.

(zu Gunther.)

> *Muß sein Tod sie betrüben,*
> *verhehlt sei ihr die That.*
> *Auf munt'res Jagen* laß morgen uns zieh'n:
> *der Edle braust uns voran, —*
> *ein Eber bracht' ihn um.*

GUNTHER und BRÜNNHILDE.

> *So soll es sein! Siegfried falle!*
> *Sühn' er die Schmach, die er mir schuf!*
> Eidtreue *hat er getrogen,*
> *mit seinem Blut büß' er die Schuld!*

HAGEN.

> So soll es sein! Siegfried falle!
> *Sterb' er dahin, der strahlende Held!*
> *Mein ist der Hort, mir muß er gehören, —*
> entrissen d'rum sei ihm der Ring!

Sechste Scene.

(Siegfried und Gudrune erscheinen an der Halle. Siegfried trägt einen Eichen-
kranz, Gudrune einen Kranz von bunten Blumen auf dem Haupte.)

SIEGFRIED.

> Was säumst du, Gunther, hier,
> lässest der Hochzeit Sorge
> mir, dem Gaste, allein?
> Hausrecht übt' ich für dich:
> von deinen Weiden zum Weihhof hin

GUNTHER

    But Gudrun, to whom I granted him!

    If we were to punish her husband so,

    How would we stand before her?

BRÜNNHILDE

(wildly)

    What did my wisdom teach me? What did runes show me?

    In my helpless misery I see clearly:

    Gudrune is the name of the magic,

    Which has taken my husband from me.

    Let fear take her!

HAGEN

(to Gunther)

    If his death would make her unhappy,

    Let the deed be hidden from her.

    Let us go on a merry hunt tomorrow:

    The noble one will rush ahead of us —

    A boar killed him.

GUNTHER and BRÜNNHILDE

    So shall it be! Let Siegfried fall!

    Let him atone for the shame he did to me!

    He has broken his oaths,

    With his blood let him repay the guilt!

HAGEN

    So shall it be! Let Siegfried fall!

    Let him die, the shining hero!

    The hoard is then mine, it must belong to me —

    Let the ring be torn from him then!

Sixth Scene

(Siegfried and Gudrune appear from the hall. Siegfried is wearing an oak wreath, Gudrune has a wreath of colorful flowers on her head.)

SIEGFRIED

    Why do you tarry here, Gunther,

    You leave attending to the wedding

    To me, the guest, alone?

    I carried out the duties of the house:

    I drove in from your meadows

starke Thiere trieb ich heim;
von Frauen nahm ich frische Kränze,
lustiger Bänder bunte Zier:
daß du den Segen sprächest,
suchen wir dich nun auf.

GUNTHER.
(mit besonnener, ruhiger Fassung.)
Wem ziemte besser wohl
des Segens Spruch als dir?
doch willst du, zeig' ich gern,
daß deiner Zucht ich weiche.
So lang' du lebest, weiß ich wohl,
daß ich dein eigen bin.

SIEGFRIED.
(ist nah' zu Gunther herangetreten.)
Zähmtest du die Wilde?

GUNTHER.
Sie schweigt.

SIEGFRIED.
Mich zürnt's,
daß ich sie schlecht getäuscht;
der Tarnhelm, dünkt mich fast,
hat halb mich nur gehehlt.
Doch Frauengroll friedet sich bald;
daß ich dir sie gewonnen, dankt sie mir noch.

GUNTHER.
Glaube, nicht bleibt — ihr Dank dir aus.

GUDRUNE.
(die sich schüchtern, aber freundlich Brünnhilde genähert hat.)
Komm, schöne Schwester,
kehre in Güte bei uns ein!
Littest durch Siegfried je du ein Leid,
ich laß es ihn büßen,
sühnt er's in Liebe nicht hold.

BRÜNNHILDE.
(mit ruhiger Kälte.)
Er sühnt es bald!

(Sie weist mit der Hand Gudrune an Siegfried.)
(Man hört den Weihgesang aus dem Hofe her.)

DIE MÄNNER.
Allvater! Waltender Gott!

    Strong animals for the sacrifice;
    I took fresh wreaths from the women,
    The colorful decoration of merry ribbons:
    We have sought you out now
    So that you can pronounce the blessing.

GUNTHER
(with a cheerful, peaceful demeanor)
    Who would be more fitting
    To pronounce the blessing than you?
    But if you wish I will gladly show
    That I give in to your breeding.
    As long as you live, I know well
    That I am your vassal.

SIEGFRIED
(comes close to Gunther)
    Could you tame the wild one?

GUNTHER
    She is silent.

SIEGFRIED
    I'm angry
    That I badly deceived her;
    The Tarnhelm, it seems to me,
    Only half hid me.
    But women's anger passes soon;
    She will come to thank me for winning her for you,.

GUNTHER
    Believe me — her thanks will come to you.

GUDRUNE
(who has approached Brünnhilde shyly but in a friendly manner)
    Come, beautiful sister,
    Take your place with us in peace!
    If you ever suffered at Siegfried's hands,
    I'll let him pay for it,
    If he doesn't pay for it with love.

BRÜNNHILDE
(with quiet coldness)
    He will pay for it soon!

(She gestures with her hand that Gudrune should go with Siegfried.)
(The song of sacrifice is heard from the courtyard.)

THE VASSALS
    All-father! Ruling god!

Allweiser! Weihlicher Hort!
Wotan! Wotan! Wende dich her!

DIE FRAUEN.

Allmilde! Mächtige Mutter!
Allgüt'ge! Freundliche Göttin!
Frikka! Frikka! Heilige Frau!

DIE MÄNNER und FRAUEN.
(zusammen.)

Weiset die herrliche, heilige Schaar,
hieher zu horchen dem Weihgesang!

(Während des Gesanges:)

SIEGFRIED.

Folgt dem Gesang! Du schreite voran.

GUNTHER.
(vor Siegfried zurücktretend.)

Dir, Siegfried, folge ich:
in deine Halle führst du Gunther,
denn dir dankt er sein Glück.

(Siegfried und Gudrune, Gunther und Brünnhilde gehen in die Halle. Hagen bleibt, ihnen nachblickend, allein zurück.)

Der Vorhang fällt.

All-wise! Holy hoard!
Wotan! Wotan! Turn to us here!
THE WOMEN
    All-generous! Mighty mother!
    All-good! Friendly goddess!
    Frikka! Frikka! Holy woman!
THE VASSALS and WOMEN
(together)
    Lead the great and holy pantheon
    Here to harken to the sacrificial song!

(During the song.)

SIEGFRIED
    Follow the song! You go ahead.
GUNTHER
(ceding the way to Siegfried)
    I follow you, Siegfried:
    You lead Gunther into your hall,
    For he owes you his good fortune.

(Siegfried and Gudrune, Gunther and Brünnhilde enter the hall. Hagen remains behind, alone, watching them.)

The curtain falls.

Dritter Akt.

(Wildes Wald- und Felsenthal am Rhein, welcher hinten an einem steilen Abhange vorbei fließt.)

Erste Scene.

(Drei Wasserjungfrauen tauchen aus dem Rheine auf und schwimmen während des folgenden Gesanges in einem Kreise umher.)

DIE DREI WASSERJUNGFRAUEN.
  Frau Sonne sendet lichte Strahlen,
  Nacht liegt in der Tiefe:
  einst war sie hell,
  da heil und hehr
  des Vaters Gold in ihr glänzte.
  Rheingold
  klares Gold,
  wie hell strahltest du einst,
  holder Stern der Tiefe!

  Frau Sonne, sende uns den Helden,
  der das Gold uns wiedergäbe!
  Ließ' er es uns,
  dein lichtes Aug'
  neideten dann wir nimmer.
  Rheingold,
  klares Gold,
  wie froh strahltest du dann,
  freier Stern der Tiefe!

(Man hört Siegfried's Horn.)

DIE ERSTE WASSERFRAU.
  Ich höre sein Horn.
DIE ZWEITE.
  Der Helde naht.
DIE DRITTE.
  Laßt uns berathen!

Third Act

(Wild forest and rocky valley on the Rhine, which flows by along a steep cliff in the rear.)

First Scene

(Three waterwomen emerge from the Rhine and swim around in a circle during the following song.)

THE THREE WATERWOMEN
    Lady Sun sends bright rays,
    Night lies in the depths:
    Once they were bright,
    Since whole and clear
    Father's gold sparkled in them.
    Rheingold
    Clear gold,
    How bright you once shone,
    Dear star of the depths!

    Lady Sun, send us the hero,
    Who will give us back the gold!
    If he were to give it to us,
    We would no longer envy
    Your bright eye.
    Rheingold
    Clear gold,
    How happy you would shine,
    Free star of the depths!

(Siegfried's horn is heard.)

THE FIRST WATERWOMAN
    I hear his horn.
THE SECOND
    The hero approaches.
THE THIRD
    Let us confer!

(Sie tauchen schnell unter.)
(Siegfried erscheint auf einer Anhöhe in vollen Waffen.)

SIEGFRIED.

> *Ein Albe führt mich irr',*
> *daß ich die Fährte verlor!*
> *He! Schelm! In welchem Berg*
> *bargst du so schnell das Wild?*

(Die Wasserfrauen tauchen wieder auf.)

DIE WASSERFRAUEN.

> *Siegfried!*

DIE DRITTE.

> *Was schiltst du in den Grund?*

DIE ZWEITE.

> *Welchem Alben bist du gram?*

DIE ERSTE.

> *Hat dich ein Nicker geneckt?*

ZU DREIEN.

> *Sag' es, Siegfried! Sag' es uns!*

SIEGFRIED.

(sie lächelnd betrachtend.)

> *Entzücktet ihr zu euch*
> *den zottigen Gesellen,*
> *der mir verschwand?*
> *Ist's euer Friedel,*
> *euch lustigen Frauen*
> *lass' ich ihn gern.*

(Die Frauen lachen laut.)

DIE ERSTE.

> *Siegfried, was giebst du uns,*
> *wenn wir das Wild dir gönnen?*

SIEGFRIED.

> *Noch bin ich beutelos,*
> *drum bittet, was ihr begehrt.*

DIE ZWEITE FRAU.

> Ein kleines Ringlein
> *glänzt dir am Finger. —*

DIE DREI ZUSAMMEN.

> *Den gieb uns!*

(They quickly dive underwater.)
(Siegfried appears on an outcropping in full weaponry.)

SIEGFRIED
 An elf misled me,
 So that I lost the path!
 Hey! Scoundrel! In which mountain
 Did you hide the game so quickly?

(The waterwomen reappear.)

THE WATERWOMEN
 Siegfried!
THE THIRD
 Why do you shout into the gorge?
THE SECOND
 Which elf made you angry?
THE FIRST
 Has a nixie teased you?
ALL THREE
 Tell us, Siegfried, Tell us!
SIEGFRIED
(smiling, he looks at them)
 Did you lure with your charms
 The shaggy fellow
 Who escaped me?
 If he's your lover,
 I'm glad to leave him to you,
 You merry women.

(The women laugh out loud.)

THE FIRST
 Siegfried, what will you give us,
 If we grant you your prey?
SIEGFRIED
 I still have caught nothing,
 So ask, whatever you desire.
THE SECOND
 A little ring
 Gleams on your finger. —
THE THREE TOGETHER
 Give that to us!

SIEGFRIED.

> *Einen Riesenwurm*
> *erschlug ich um den* Ring:
> *für des schlechten Bären Tatzen*
> *böt' ich ihn nun zum Tausch?*

DIE ERSTE FRAU.

> *Bist du so karg?*

DIE ZWEITE.

> *So geizig beim Kauf?*

DIE DRITTE.

> *Freigiebig solltest Frauen du sein!*

SIEGFRIED.

> *Verzehrt' ich an euch mein Gut,*
> *das zürnte mir wohl mein Weib.*

DIE ERSTE FRAU.

> *Sie ist wohl schlimm?*

DIE ZWEITE.

> *Sie schlägt dich wohl?*

DIE DRITTE.

> *Ihre Hand fühlt schon der Held!*

(Sie lachen.)

SIEGFRIED.

> *Nun lacht nur lustig zu,*
> *in Harm lass' ich euch doch:*
> *denn giert ihr nach dem Ring,*
> *euch Neckern geb' ich ihn nie.*

DIE ERSTE FRAU.

> *So schön!*

DIE ZWEITE.

> *So stark!*

DIE DRITTE.

> *So gehrenswerth!*

DIE DREI ZUSAMMEN.

> *Wie Schade, daß er geizig ist!*

(Sie lachen und tauchen unter.)

SIEGFRIED.
(tiefer in den Grund hinabsteigend.)

> *Was leid' ich doch das karge Lob?*
> *lass' ich so mich schmähen? —*

SIEGFRIED

    I killed a giant dragon

    To gain the ring:

    For the worthless paws of a bear

    Should I now offer it in exchange?

THE FIRST

    Are you so mean?

THE SECOND

    So stingy in exchange?

THE THIRD

    You should be generous with women!

SIEGFRIED

    If I were to waste my possessions on you,

    My wife would be angry with me.

THE FIRST

    Is she mean?

THE SECOND

    Probably she beats you?

THE THIRD

    The hero has already felt her hand!

(They laugh.)

SIEGFRIED

    Now laugh merrily away,

    I'll still leave you in grief:

    For if you desire the ring

    I'll never give it to you teasers.

THE FIRST

    So handsome!

THE SECOND

    So strong!

THE THIRD

    So desirable.

ALL THREE TOGETHER

    Too bad that he's stingy.

(They laugh and submerge.)

SIEGFRIED

(climbing down deeper into the ravine)

    Why do I suffer such grudging praise?

    Should I allow myself to be shamed so? —

> *Kämen sie wieder zum Wasserrand,*
> *den Ring könnten sie haben. —*
> *He he! Ihr muntern Wasserminnen!*
> *Kommt rasch, ich schenk' euch den Ring.*

(Die Wasserfrauen tauchen wieder auf. — Sie zeigen eine ernste, feierliche Gebärde.)

DIE WASSERFRAUEN.
> *Behalt' ihn, Held, und wahr' ihn wohl,*
> *bis dir das Unheil kund,*
> *das in dem Ring du hegst!*
> *Froh fühlst du dich dann,*
> *befrei'n wir dich von dem Fluch.*

SIEGFRIED.
(gelassen den Ring wieder ansteckend.)
> *Nun singet, was ihr wißt!*

DIE DREI WASSERFRAUEN.
(einzeln und zusammen.)
> *Siegfried! Siegfried!*
> *Schlimmes wissen wir dir.*
> *Zu deinem Verderben wahrst du den Ring!*
> *Aus des Rheines Gold ist der Ring geglüht:*
> *der ihn listig geschmiedet und schmählich verlor,*
> *der verfluchte ihn, in fernster Zeit*
> *zu zeugen den Tod dem, der ihn trüg'.*
> *Wie den Wurm du fälltest, so fällst auch du,*
> *und heute noch — so heißen wir dir's —*
> *tauschest den Ring du uns nicht,*
> *im tiefen Rhein ihn zu bergen:*
> *nur seine Fluth sühnet den Fluch.*

SIEGFRIED.
> *Ihr listigen Frauen, lasset ab!*
> *Traut' ich kaum eurem Schmeicheln,*
> *euer Schrecken trügt mich nicht.*

DIE WASSERFRAUEN.
> *Siegfried! Siegfried! Wir weisen dich wahr!*
> *Weich' aus! Weich' aus dem Fluche!*
> *Ihn flochten webende Nornen*
> *in des Urgesetzes Seil.*

If they came back to the water's edge,
They could have the ring. —
Hey! Hey! You merry mermaids
Come quickly, I'll give you the ring.

(The waterwomen emerge again. They show a serious, solemn
expression.)

THE WATERWOMEN
    Keep it, hero, and protect it well,
    Until you experience the catastrophe,
    That you hold in the ring.
    You would be happy then,
    If we were to free you from the curse.
SIEGFRIED
(casually putting the ring back on)
    Now sing what you know!
THE THREE WATERWOMEN
(singly and together)
    Siegfried! Siegfried!
    We know evil things about you.
    You keep the ring to your own ruin!
    The ring was forged from the Rhine's gold:
    The one who cunningly forged it and shamefully lost it,
    He cursed it in days long past
    So that it would bring death to the one who wore it.
    Just as you felled the dragon, you will also fall,
    Still today — we promise you that —
    If you do not exchange the ring to us,
    So that we can preserve it deep in the Rhine:
    Only its flood can end the curse.
SIEGFRIED
    You cunning women, leave off!
    I scarcely trusted your flattery,
    Your fearmongering doesn't deceive me.
THE WATERWOMEN
    Siegfried! Siegfried! What we foretell is true!
    Avoid it! Avoid the curse!
    It was woven by weaving Norns
    Into the rope of eternal law.

SIEGFRIED.

    Eurem Fluche fliehe ich nicht,

    noch weich' ich der Nornen Gewebe!

    Wozu mein Muth mich mahnt,

    das ist mir Urgesetz, —

    und was mein Sinn mir ersieht,

    das ist mir so bestimmt.

    Sagt denen, die euch gesandt:

    dem Zagen schneidet kein Schwert,

    dem Starken nur frommt seine Schärfe, —

    ihm woll' es Keiner entwinden!

DIE FRAUEN.

    Weh'! Siegfried!

    Wo Götter trauern, trotzest du?

SIEGFRIED.

    Dämmert der Tag auf jener Haide,

    wo sorgend die Helden sie schaaren, —

    entbrennt der Kampf, dem die Nornen selbst

    das Ende nicht wissen zu künden:

    nach meinem Muth

    entscheid' ich den Sieg!

    Nun sollt' ich selbst mich entmannen,

    mit dem Ring verthun meinen Muth?

    Faßte er nicht meines Fingers Werth,

    den Reif geb' ich nicht fort:

    denn das Leben — seht! — so —

    werf' ich es weit von mir!

(Er hat mit den letzten Worten eine Erdscholle vom Boden aufgehoben und über sein Haupt hinter sich geworfen.)

DIE WASSERFRAUEN.

    Kommt, Schwestern! Schwindet dem Thoren!

    So stark und weise wähnt' er sich,

    als gebunden und blind er ist.

    Eide schwur er und weiß sie nicht:

    Runen weiß er und kennt sie nicht:

    ein hehrstes Gut ward ihm gegönnt,

    daß er's verworfen, weiß er nicht:

    nur den Ring, der Tod ihm bringt,

    den Reif nur will er behalten!

    Leb' wohl, Siegfried!

    Ein stolzes Weib

SIEGFRIED

    I won't flee your curse,

    Nor will I give in to the Norn's weaving!

    Whatever my courage tells me

    Is eternal law to me —

    And whatever my senses tell me,

    That is fated for me.

    Tell those who have sent you:

    No sword can cut for a coward,

    Only the strong can make use of its sharpness —

    No one will be able to steal it.

THE THREE WATERWOMEN

    Woe! Siegfried!

    Where gods mourn, you resist?

SIEGFRIED

    When the day dawns on that heath,

    Where the heroes assemble in distress —

    When the battle erupts, of which even the Norns

    Cannot determine the end:

    According to my courage

    I'll determine the victory!

    Should I now unman myself,

    Give away my courage with the ring?

    If it held no more than my finger's value,

    I would not give up the ring:

    Because — behold — life itself — thus

    I throw far from me!

(With the last words, he picks up a clod of earth from the ground and throws it over his head behind him.)

THE THREE WATERWOMEN

    Come sisters! Leave the fool!

    He considers himself as strong and wise,

    As in reality he is bound and blind.

    He swore oaths, and does not know them:

    He learned runes and doesn't remember them:

    The highest possession was granted him,

    And he doesn't know that he has thrown it away.

    Only the ring, which will bring him death,

    Only that ring he wants to keep!

    Farewell, Siegfried!

    A proud woman

wird heute noch dich *beerben:*
sie giebt *uns besser Gehör.*
Zu ihr! Zu ihr! Zu ihr!

(Sie schwimmen singend davon.)

SIEGFRIED.
(sieht ihnen lachend nach.)
    Im Wasser wie am Lande
    lernt' ich nun Weiberart:
    wer nicht ihrem Schmeicheln traut,
    den schrecken sie mit Droh'n:
    wer dem nun kühnlich trotzt,
    dem kommt dann ihr Keifen dran. —
    Und doch, trüg' ich nicht Gudrun Treu',
    der zieren Frauen eine
    hätt' ich mir frisch gezähmt.

(Jagdhornrufe kommen von der Höhe näher: Siegfried antwortet lustig auf seinem Horne.)

Zweite Scene.

(Gunther, Hagen und die Mannen kommen während des Folgenden von der Höhe herab.)

HAGEN.
(noch auf der Höhe.)
    Hoiho!
SIEGFRIED.
    Hoiho!
DIE MANNEN.
    Hoiho!

HAGEN.
    Finden wir endlich, wohin du flogst?
SIEGFRIED.
    Kommt herab, hier ist frisch und kühl!

Will inherit from you today:
She will listen to us better.
To her! To her! To her!

(They swim away singing.)

SIEGFRIED
(watches them and laughs)
 On water and on land
 I have learned women's ways:
 If you do not believe their flattery,
 Then they frighten you with threats:
 If you boldly stand up to them,
 Then they begin to nag —
 And still, if I were not true to Gudrun,
 I would have quickly tamed
 One of the shapely women.

(Hunting horns approach from the heights: Siegfried answers merrily on his horn.)

Second Scene

(Gunther, Hagen, and the vassals come down, during the following scene, from the heights.)

HAGEN
(still on the heights)
 Hoiho!
SIEGFRIED
 Hoiho!
THE VASSALS
 Hoiho!

HAGEN
 Have we finally found where you fled?
SIEGFRIED
 Come down, here it is fresh and cool!

HAGEN.

> *Hier rasten wir und rüsten das Mahl.*
> *Laßt ruh'n die Beute und bietet die Schläuche!*

(Jagdbeute wird zu Haufen gelegt, Trinkhörner und Schläuche werden hervorgeholt. Später lagert sich Alles.)

HAGEN.

> *Der uns das Wild verscheucht,*
> *nun sollt ihr Wunder schauen,*
> *was Siegfried sich erjagt!*

SIEGFRIED.
(lachend.)

> *Schlimm steht's um mein Mahl!*
> *Von eurer Beute bitt' ich für mich.*

HAGEN.

> *Du beuteleer?*

SIEGFRIED.

> *Auf Waldjagd zog ich aus,*
> *doch Wasserwild zeigte sich nur:*
> *war ich dazu recht berathen,*
> *drei wilde Wasservögel*
> *hätt' ich euch gefangen,*
> *die dort auf dem Rheine mir sangen:*
> *erschlagen würd' ich noch heut'!*

(Gunther erschrickt und blickt düster auf Hagen.)

HAGEN.

> *Das wäre böse Jagd,*
> *wenn den Beutelosen selbst*
> *ein lauernd Wild erlegte!*

SIEGFRIED.

> *Mich dürstet!*

(Er hat sich zwischen Hagen und Gunther gelagert; gefüllte Trinkhörner werden ihnen gereicht.)

HAGEN.

> *Ich hörte sagen, Siegfried,*
> *der Vögel Sangessprache*
> *verstündest du wohl: — so wär' das wahr?*

HAGEN

> Here we shall rest and prepare the meal.
> Let the booty rest and offer the wineskins!

(The hunting booty is piled in a heap. Drinking horns and skins are brought forth. Later everyone is lying down.)

HAGEN

> The one who has driven away our game.
> Now you will all hear marvels
> of what Siegfried has hunted down.

SIEGFRIED

(laughing)

> It won't do well for my meal!
> I'll have to beg something from yours.

HAGEN

> You with no booty?

SIEGFRIED

> I set out on a forest hunt,
> But I saw only water fowl:
> If I had been properly prepared
> Three wild water birds
> I would have caught for you,
> Which sang to me here in the Rhine
> That I would be killed today!

(Gunther is startled and looks darkly at Hagen.)

HAGEN

> That would be an evil hunt,
> If even the one without booty
> Should fall to a lurking wild animal!

SIEGFRIED

> I'm thirsty!

(He has taken his place between Hagen and Gunther. Filled drinking horns are passed to them.)

HAGEN

> I've heard it told, Siegfried,
> That you could understand
> The birds' singing language — is that true?

SIEGFRIED.

> *Seit lange acht' ich* ihrer *nicht mehr.*

(Er trinkt und reicht sein Horn Gunther.)

> *Trink', Gunther, trink'!*
> *Dein Bruder bringt es dir.*

GUNTHER.

(gedankenvoll und schwermüthig in das Horn blickend.)

> *Du mischtest matt und bleich:*
> *dein Blut allein darin!*

SIEGFRIED.

(lachend.)

> *So misch' es mit dem deinen!*

(Er gießt aus Gunther's Horn in das seine, so daß es überläuft.)

> *Nun floß gemischt es über!*
> *Lass' das* den Göttern *Labsal sein!*

GUNTHER.

(seufzend.)

> *Du überfroher Held!*

SIEGFRIED.

(leise zu Hagen.)

> *Ihm macht Brünnhilde Müh'?*

HAGEN.

> *Verstünd' er sie so gut,*
> *wie du der Vögel Gesang!*

SIEGFRIED.

> *Seit Frauen ich singen hörte,*
> *vergaß ich ihrer ganz.*

HAGEN.

> *Doch einst vernahmst du sie?*

SIEGFRIED.

> *Hei, Gunther! Ungemuther Mann!*
> *Dankst du es mir, so sing' ich die Mären*
> *aus meinen jungen Tagen.*

GUNTHER.

> *Die hör' ich gern.*

HAGEN.

> *So singe, edler Held!*

(Alles lagert sich nah' um Siegfried, welcher allein aufrecht sitzt, während die Anderen tiefer gestreckt liegen.)

SIEGFRIED

For a long time I've paid them no more heed.

(He drinks and passes his horn to Gunther.)

Drink, Gunther, Drink!
Your brother brings it to you.
GUNTHER
(thoughtful and miserable he looks into the horn)
You mixed it flat and pale:
Only your blood is in it!
SIEGFRIED
(laughing)
So mix it with yours!

(He pours Gunther's horn into his, so that it overflows.)

Now it mixes together and overflows!
Let it be a tonic for the gods!
GUNTHER
(sighing)
You far too joyful hero!
SIEGFRIED
(softly to Hagen)
Brünnhilde is giving him trouble?
HAGEN
If only he understood her as well
As you did the birds' song.
SIEGFRIED
Since I heard women singing,
I forgot them completely.
HAGEN
But you did understand them once?
SIEGFRIED
Hey, Gunther! Dejected man!
Would you thank me, if I sing stories
From my youthful days?
GUNTHER
I would be glad to hear them.
HAGEN
So sing, noble hero!

(Everyone lies close to Siegfried, who alone is sitting up, while the others lie
on the ground.)

SIEGFRIED.

Mime hieß ein mannlicher *Zwerg,*
zierlich und scharf wußt' er zu schmieden:
Sieglind, meiner lieben Mutter,
half er im wilden Walde:
den sie sterbend da gebar,
mich Starken zog er auf
mit klugem Zwergenrath.
Meines Vaters Tod that er mir kund,
gab mir die Stücken seines Schwertes,
das in letzter Schlacht er zerschlagen:
als Meister lehrte Mime mich schmieden,
des Schwertes Stücken schmolz ich ein,
und Balmung schuf ich mir neu.
Balmung hämmert' ich hart und fest,
bis kein Fehl mehr an ihm zu erspäh'n:
einen Ambos mußt' er mir spellen.
Da däuchte nun Mime tüchtig die Wehr,
daß mit ihr einen Wurm ich erschlüg',
der auf schlimmer Haide sich wand: —
"Wie lachten wohl — sagt' ich — Hunding's Söhne,
hörten sie solch' ein Lied,
daß Siegfried's Waffe mit Würrmern focht,
eh' sie den Vater gerächt!"

HAGEN.

Dess' wird dir nun Lob!

DIE MANNEN.

Lob sei dir, Siegfried!

(Sie trinken.)

SIEGFRIED.

Da heerte Balmung, mein hartes Schwert,
die Hundinge sanken vor ihm.
Nun folgt' ich Mime, den Wurm zu fällen,
ihm wühlt' ich im riesigen Wanst: —
jetzt aber höret Wunder!
Von des Wurmes Blut mir brannten die Finger,
sie führt' ich kühlend zum Mund:
kaum netzt' ein wenig die Zunge das Naß,
was da die Vögelein sangen,
das konnt' ich flug's versteh'n;
auf Ästen sie saßen und sagten:

SIEGFRIED

    There was a man-like dwarf named Mime
    Who could forge fine and sharp things:
    Sieglind, my dear mother,
    He helped in the wild forest:
    The one she gave birth to there while dying,
    Me, the strong one he raised,
    With cunning dwarfish lore.
    He told me of my father's death,
    He gave me the pieces of his sword,
    Which had been broken in his last battle:
    As master Mime taught me to forge,
    I melted together the broken pieces
    And made Balmung new.
    Balmung I hammered hard and firm,
    Until no flaw could be seen in it:
    It had to split me an anvil.
    Mime then felt the weapon good enough
    That I could kill a dragon with it
    Which was coiling on an evil heath —
    "How they would laugh — I said — Hunding's sons,
    If they heard such a song,
    That Siegfried's weapon had fought with dragons
    Before it avenged the father!"

HAGEN

    That earns you praise!

THE VASSALS

    Praise to you, Siegfried.

(They drink.)

SIEGFRIED

    Balmung, my hard sword, harried there,
    The Hundings sank before it.
    Now I followed Mime, to fell the dragon,
    I ripped through his mighty hide —
    Now hear amazing things!
    My finger burned from the dragon's blood,
    I put in my mouth to cool:
    Scarcely had the moisture touched my tongue,
    I could immediately understand everything
    The birds were singing there;
    They sat on the branches and said:

>*Hei, Siegfried gehört nun der Niblungenhort!*
O, traut' er Mime, dem Treulosen, nicht!
Ihm sollt' er den Schatz *nur gewinnen,*
jetzt lauert er listig am Weg;
nach dem Leben trachtet er Siegfried,
O traute Siegfried nicht Mime!«

HAGEN.

Sie warnten dich gut.

DIE MANNEN.

Vergaltest du Mime?

SIEGFRIED.

Zu mir zwang ich den listigen Zwerg:
Ihn mußte Balmung erlegen.
Nun lauscht' ich wieder den Waldvögelein,
wie sie lustig sangen und sprachen:
»*Hei, Siegfried erschlug nun den schlimmen Zwerg;*
o fänd' in der Höhle den Hort er jetzt!
Wollt' er den Tarnhelm gewinnen,
der taugt' ihm zu wonniger That;
doch möcht' *er den Ring sich errathen,*
der macht' ihn zum Walter der Welt.«

HAGEN.

Ring und Tarnhelm trugst du nun heim.

DIE MANNEN.

Die Vögelein hörtest du wieder?

HAGEN.

(nachdem er den Saft eines Krautes in das Trinkhorn ausgedrückt.)

Trink' erst, Held, aus meinem Horn!
Ich würzte dir holden Trank,
die Erinnerung hell dir zu wecken,
daß Fernes nicht dir entfalle.

SIEGFRIED.

(nachdem er getrunken.)

Und wieder lauscht' ich den Waldvögelein,
wie sie lustig sangen und sprachen: —
»*Hei, Siegfried gehört nun der Helm und der Ring;*
jetzt wüßten wir ihm noch das herrlichste Weib!
Auf hohem Felsen sie schläft,
ein Feuer umbrennt ihren Saal:
durchschritt' er die Gluth, *erweckt' er die Braut,*
Brünnhilde wäre dann sein!«

(Gunther hört mit immer wachsendem Erstaunen zu.)

"Hey, Siegfried now owns the hoard of the Niblungs!
If only he wouldn't trust Mime, the faithless one!
He was only supposed to win the hoard for him.
Now he cunningly waits in ambush:
He plots to take Siegfried's life,
If only Siegfried wouldn't trust Mime!"

HAGEN

They warned you well.

THE VASSALS

Did you repay Mime?

SIEGFRIED

I forced the cunning dwarf to come to me:
Balmung brought him down.
Now I listened again to the forest birds,
As they sang merrily and said:
"Hey, Siegfried has now slain the evil dwarf;
If only he would find the hoard in the cave!
If only he would take the Tarnhelm,
It would serve him for wonderful deeds;
But if he could find the ring,
It would make him the lord of the world.'

HAGEN

Then you took away the ring and the Tarnhelm.

THE VASSALS

You heard the birds again?

HAGEN

(after squeezing the juice of an herb into the drinking horn)
Drink, hero, from my horn!
I spiced a fine drink for you,
To awaken all memories for you.
So that you won't forget distant things.

SIEGFRIED

(after drinking)
And again I listened to the forest birds,
As they merrily sang and said:
"Hey, Siegfried now owns the helm and the ring;
Now we know of the most magnificent woman for him!
She sleeps on high rocks,
A fire surrounds her hall:
If he strides through the flames and awakens the bride,
Brünnhilde would then be his!"

(Gunther listens with growing astonishment.)

HAGEN.

Und folgtest du der Vögelein Rath?

SIEGFRIED.

Rasch ohne Zaudern zog ich nun aus,
bis den feurigen Felsen ich traf;
durch die Lohe schritt ich und fand zum Lohn
schlafend ein wonniges Weib
in lichter Waffen Gewand:
zur Seite ihr ruhte ein Roß,
in Schlaf versenkt wie sie.
Den Helm löst' ich der herrlichen Maid,
mein Kuß erweckte sie kühn:
o wie mich selig da umschlang
der schönen Brünnhilde Arm!

GUNTHER.

Was hör' ich?

(Zwei Raben fliegen aus einem Busche auf, kreisen über Siegfried und fliegen davon.)

HAGEN.

Verstehst *du auch dieser Raben* Spruch?

(Siegfried fährt heftig auf und blickt, Hagen den Rücken wendend, den Raben nach.)

HAGEN.

Sie eilen, Wotan dich zu melden!

(Er stößt seinen Speer in Siegfried's Rücken; Gunther fällt ihm, zu spät, in den Arm.)

GUNTHER und DIE MANNEN.

Hagen, was thust du?

SIEGFRIED.

(schwingt mit beiden Händen seinen Schild hoch empor, Hagen damit zu zerschmettern: die Kraft verläßt ihn und krachend stürzt er über den Schild zusammen.)

HAGEN.

(auf den zu Boden Gestreckten deutend.)

Meineid rächt' ich an ihm!

HAGEN

And did you follow the birds' advice?

SIEGFRIED

Quickly, without hesitation I set out,

Until I found the fiery rock;

I went through the flames and found as reward

Sleeping a wonderful woman

Clothed in bright armor:

Beside her rested a steed,

Deep in sleep as she was.

I loosened the helmet on the wonderful maiden,

A kiss awakened her boldly:

Oh! how happily I was embraced

In beautiful Brünnhilde's arms!

GUNTHER

What do I hear?

(Two ravens fly up from a bush, circle around Siegfried and then fly away.)

HAGEN

Do you also understand also the language of these ravens?

(Siegfried springs up and stares after the ravens with his back to Hagen.)

HAGEN

They hurry to announce you to Wotan!

(He thrusts his spear into Siegfried's back; Gunther grabs his arms but too late.)

GUNTHER and THE VASSALS

Hagen, what are you doing?

SIEGFRIED

(Raises his shield with both hands to crush Hagen with it: but the strength leaves him and he collapses noisily onto the shield.)

HAGEN

(pointing to the man lying on the ground)

I avenged perjury on him!

(Er wendet sich ruhig zur Seite ab und verliert sich dann einsam über die Höhe, wo man ihn langsam von dannen schreiten sieht.)
(Lange Stille der tiefsten Erschütterung.)

GUNTHER.
(beugt sich schmerzlich zu Siegfried's Seite nieder; die Mannen umstehen teilnahmvoll den Sterbenden.)
(Dämmerung ist bereits mit der Erscheinung der Raben hereingebrochen.)
SIEGFRIED.
(noch einmal die Augen glanzvoll aufschlagend, mit feierlicher Stimme.)
    Brünnhild! Brünnhild!
    Du strahlendes Wotanskind!
    Hell leuchtend durch die Nacht
    seh' ich dem Helden dich nah'n:
    mit heilig ernstem Lächeln
    rüstest du dein Roß,
    das thautriefend
    die Lüfte durchläuft.
    Hieher den Kämpfeweiser!
    Hier giebt es Wal zu küren!
    Mich Glücklichen, den du zum Gatten korst,
    nach Walhall weise mich nun, —
    daß zu aller Helden Ehre
    Allvaters Meth ich trinke,
    den du, wunschliche Maid,
    minnig dem Trauten reichst!
    Brünnhild! Brünnhild! Sei gegrüßt!

(Er stirbt. Die Mannen erheben die Leiche auf den Schild und geleiten sie in feierlichem Zuge über die Felsenhöhe langsam von dannen. Gunther folgt der Leiche zunächst. Der Mond bricht durch die Wolken und beleuchtet auf der Höhe den Trauerzug der Mannen. — Dann steigen Nebel aus dem Rhein auf und erfüllen allmählich die ganze Bühne bis nach vorn. — Sobald sich dann die Nebel wieder zertheilen, erblickt man —)

Dritte Scene.

(— die Halle der Gibichungen mit dem Uferraum, wie im ersten Akte. — Nacht. Mondschein spiegelt sich im Rheine. Gudrune tritt aus ihrem Gemache in die Halle heraus.)

(He quietly turns away and disappears alone over the heights, where he can be seen striding away slowly.)
(Long silence of deepest shock.)

GUNTHER
(leans painfully over Siegfried; the vassals surround the dying man sympathetically.)
(Dusk has fallen with the appearance of the ravens.)
SIEGFRIED
(opening his eyes gloriously, with a solemn voice)
> Brünnhild! Brünnhild
> You radiant child of Wotan!
> Brightly shining through the night
> I see the hero approaching you:
> With a serious, holy smile
> You saddle your horse,
> Which runs through the skies
> dripping dew.
> Let the ruler of battles come here!
> Here there are dead to choose!
> Me, fortunate one, whom you chose as husband,
> Lead me now to Valhalla —
> So that in honor of all heroes
> I can drink all-father's mead,
> Which you, maiden of desire,
> Lovingly bring to the beloved!
> Brünnhild! Brünnhild! My greetings to you!

(He dies. The vassals lift the corpse onto his shield and carry it in a solemn procession slowly away over the heights. Gunther follows immediately after the corpse. The moon breaks through the clouds and and illuminates the funeral procession of the vassals. — Then fog rises from the Rhine and gradually fills the whole stage to the front. — As soon as the fog lifts, one sees —)

Third Scene

(— the hall of the Gibichungs with the banks of the Rhine as in the first act. — Night. Moonlight is mirrored in the Rhine. Gudrune emerges from her chamber into the hall.)

GUDRUNE.
> *War das sein Horn?* —

(Sie lauscht.)

> *Nein! Noch kehrt er nicht heim.* —
> *Schlimme Träume* hab' ich geträumt! —
> Wild hört' ich wiehern sein Roß, —
> *Lachen Brünnhilde's weckte mich auf.*
> *— Wer war das Weib,*
> *das ich zum* Rheine *schreiten sah?* —
> *Ich fürchte Brünnhild; — ist sie daheim?*

(Sie lauscht an einer Thüre rechts, und ruft dann leise.)

> *Brünnhild! — Brünnhild! — bist du wach?*

(Sie öffnet schüchtern und blickt hinein.)

> *Leer das Gemach! — so war es sie,*
> *die zum Rhein ich* wandeln *sah?* —

(Sie erschrickt und lauscht nach der Ferne.)

> Hört' ich ein *Horn? — Nein, öde Alles:* — —
> Kehrte Siegfried nun bald heim!

(Sie wendet sich mit einigen Schritten ihrem Gemache zu; als sie Hagen's Stimme vernimmt, hält sie an und bleibt vor Furcht gefesselt eine Zeitlang unbeweglich stehen.)

HAGEN'S STIMME.
(von außen sich nähernd.)
> *Hoiho! Hoiho! Wacht auf! Wacht auf!*
> *Lichte! Lichte! Helle Brände!*
> *Jagdbeute bringen wir heim!*
> *Hoiho! Hoiho!*

(Licht und wachsender Feuerschein von außen rechts.)

HAGEN.
(in die Halle tretend.)
> *Auf, Gudrune! Begrüße Siegfried!*
> *Der starke Held, er kehret heim!*

GUDRUNE
> Was that his horn? —

(She listens.)

> No! He still hasn't returned home. —
> I have dreamed bad dreams! —
> I heard his steed neighing wildly, —
> Brünnhilde's laughter awakened me.
> — Who was the woman
> That I saw walking toward the Rhine? —
> I fear Brünnhild — is she at home?

(She listens at a door on the right, and calls softly.)

> Brünnhild! — Brünnhild! — Are you awake?

(She opens it shyly and looks inside.)

> The chamber is empty. — so it was she
> I saw walking to the Rhine? —

(She is startled and listens for distant sounds.)

> Did I hear a horn? — no, everything is deserted: — —
> If only Siegfried would return soon!

(She turns back several steps toward her chamber. When she hears Hagen's voice, she stops and remains standing motionless and fettered by fear.)

HAGEN'S VOICE
(approaching from outside)
> Hoiho! Hoiho! Awaken! Awaken!
> Lights! Lights! Bright torches!
> We bring hunting booty home!
> Hoiho! Hoiho!

(Light and increasing firelight from offstage right.)

HAGEN
(striding into the hall)
> Arise Gudrune! Greet Siegfried!
> The strong hero, he returns home!

(Mannen und Frauen geleiten in großer Verwirrung mit Lichten und Feuerbränden den Zug der mit Siegfried's Leiche Heimkehrenden, unter denen Gunther.)

GUDRUNE.
(in höchster Angst.)
>   *Was geschah, Hagen?* Sein Horn hört' ich nicht!

HAGEN.
>   *Der bleiche Held, nicht bläst er's mehr, —*
>   *nicht stürmt er zum Jagen, zum Streit nicht mehr,*
>   *noch wirbt er um wonnige Frauen!*

GUDRUNE.
(mit wachsendem Entsetzen.)
>   *Was bringen die?*

HAGEN.
>   *Eines wilden Eber's Beute:*
>   *Siegfried, deinen todten Mann!*

GUDRUNE.
(schreit auf und stürzt über die Leiche hin, welche in der Mitte der Halle niedergesetzt ist. — Allgemeine Erschütterung und Trauer.)

GUNTHER.
(indem er die Ohnmächtige aufzurichten sucht.)
>   *Gudrune, holde Schwester!*
>   *Hebe dein Aug', schweige mir nicht!*

GUDRUNE.
(wieder erwachend.)
>   *Siegfried! — Siegfried — erschlagen!*

(Sie stößt Gunther heftig zurück.)

>   *Fort, treuloser Bruder!*
>   *Du Mörder meines Mannes!*
>   *O Hülfe! Hülfe! Weh'! Weh'!*
>   Siegfried haben sie erschlagen!

GUNTHER.
>   *Nicht klage wider mich!*
>   *Dort klage wider Hagen!*
>   *Er ist der verfluchte Eber,*
>   *der deinen Mann zerfleischt!*

HAGEN.
>   *Bist du mir gram darum?*

GUNTHER.
>   *Angst und Unheil greife dich immer!*

(Vassals and women accompany with lights and torches in great
confusion the procession of those bearing Siegfried's corpse, among
them Gunther.)

GUDRUNE
(in highest anxiety)
    What happened Hagen! I didn't hear his horn!
HAGEN
    The pale hero will not blow it again —
    Nor will he rush to the hunt or to battle again,
    Nor will he woo beautiful women!
GUDRUNE
(with growing shock)
    What are they bringing?
HAGEN
    The victim of a wild boar:
    Siegfried, your dead husband!
GUDRUNE
(screams and falls over the corpse, which has been laid down in the middle of
the hall. — General shock and grief.)
GUNTHER
(attempting to raise his unconscious sister)
    Gudrune, dear sister!
    Lift your eyes, do not remain silent.
GUDRUNE
(coming to herself)
    Siegfried — Siegfried — slain!

(She pushes Gunther rudely away.)

    Away, faithless brother!
    You murderer of my husband!
    O Help! Help! Woe! Woe!
    They have killed Siegfried!
GUNTHER
    Do not accuse me!
    Accuse Hagen there!
    He is the accursed boar
    Who tore apart your husband!
HAGEN
    Do you hold that against me?
GUNTHER
    Let fear and ill-luck follow you forever!

HAGEN.
(mit furchtbarem Trotze herantretend.)
> *Ja denn, ich hab' ihn erschlagen,*
> *ich, Hagen, schlug ihn zu todt:*
> *meinem Speere war er gespart,*
> *bei dem er Meineid sprach.*
> *Heiliges Beuterecht*
> *hab' ich mir nun errungen:*
> *drum fordr' ich hier diesen Ring!*

GUNTHER.
> *Zurück! was mir verfiel,*
> *sollst nimmer du empfah'n!*

HAGEN.
> *Ihr Mannen, richtet mein Recht!*

GUNTHER.
> *Rührst du an Gudrun's Erbe,*
> *schamloser Albensohn?*

HAGEN.
(das Schwert ziehend.)
> *Des Alben Erbe fordert so — sein Sohn:*

(Er dringt auf Gunther ein; dieser wehrt sich: sie fechten. Die Mannen werfen sich dazwischen. Gunther fällt von einem Streiche Hagen's todt darnieder.)

HAGEN.
> *Her den Ring!*

(Er greift nach Siegfried's Hand, diese hebt sich drohend empor.)
(Allgemeines Entsetzen. Gudrune schreit laut auf.)

DIE MANNEN und FRAUEN.
> Weh'! Weh'!

HAGEN
(approaching with terrifying hostility)
>Yes then, I slew him.
>I, Hagen, struck him dead:
>He was destined for my spear,
>On which he swore falsely.
>I have now earned
>The holy right of booty;
>Therefore I demand this ring!

GUNTHER
>Back! You should never receive
>What I have inherited.

HAGEN
>You vassals, judge my right!

GUNTHER
>Do you dare touch Gudrune's inheritance,
>Shameless son of an elf?

HAGEN
(drawing his sword)
>The elf's heritage demands thus — his son:

(He attacks Gunther, who defends himself: they fight. The vassals throw themselves between them. Gunther falls dead from a stroke of Hagen's sword.)

HAGEN
>Give the ring here!

(He reaches for Siegfried's hand, which rises in a threatening gesture.)
(General shock. Gudrune screams aloud.)

THE VASSALS and WOMEN
>Woe! Woe!

Vierte Scene.

(Vom Hintergrunde her schreitet Brünnhilde fest und feierlich nach dem Vordergrunde zu.)

BRÜNNHILDE.
(noch im Hintergrunde.)
    Schweigt euren Jammer, eure eitle Wuth!
    Hier steht sein Weib, *das ihr alle verriethet.*

(Sie schreitet ruhig weiter vor.)

    Kinder hör' ich greinen,
    da süße Milch sie verschüttet:
    nicht hört' ich *würdige Klage,*
    wie sie *des Helden werth.*
GUDRUNE.
    Brünnhilde! Unheilvolle!
    Du brachtest uns diese Noth!
    Die du ihm die Männer verhetztest,
    weh'! daß du dem Hause genaht!
BRÜNNHILDE.
    Armselige, schweig'!
    Nie warst du sein Eheweib.
    Sein Gemahl *bin ich,* dem er Eide *schwur,*
    eh' Siegfried je dich ersah.
GUDRUNE.
(in heftigster Verzweiflung.)
    Verfluchter Hagen! Weh'! Ach weh',
    daß du den Trank mir riethest,
    der ihr den Gatten entrückt.
    O Jammer! Jammer! nun weiß ich, ach!
    daß Brünnhild die Traute war,
    die durch den Trank er vergaß!

(Sie wendet sich voll Scheu von Siegfried ab und beugt sich in Schmerz aufgelöst über Gunther's Leiche, in welcher Stellung sie bis an das Ende verweilt. — Langes Schweigen. — Hagen steht, auf Speer und Schild gelehnt, in finsteres, trotziges Sinnen versunken, an der äußersten Seite, derjenigen entgegengesetzt, auf welcher Gudrune über Gunther hingestreckt liegt. Brünnhilde bei Siegfried's Leiche in der Mitte.)

Fourth Scene

(From the background Brünnhilde strides purposefully and solemnly toward the front.)

BRÜNNHILDE
(still in the background)
    Silence your grief, your idle anger!
    Here stands his wife, whom you all betrayed.

(She steps quietly forward.)

    I heard children whining,
    Because they had spilled sweet milk:
    I did not hear a noble lament,
    That would be worthy of a hero.
GUDRUNE
    Brünnhilde! Bringer of misfortune!
    You brought us this strife!
    You urged the men on against him
    Woe! That you ever came near this house.
BRÜNNHILDE
    Poor woman, be silent!
    You were never his wife.
    I am his spouse, to whom he swore oaths.
    Before Siegfried ever saw you.
GUDRUNE
(in the highest desperation)
    Accursed Hagen! Woe! O Woe,
    That you advised me to give Siegfried the potion
    That took away her husband.
    O misery, misery! Now I understand.
    Brünnhilde was the beloved
    the drink caused him to forget.

(She turns fearfully away from Siegfried and bends full of grief over Gunther's body, where she remains until the end.— long silence. — Hagen stands, leaning on his spear and shield, sunken in hostile thought, on the opposite side from where Gudrune is stretched out over Gunther's body. Brünnhilde next to Siegfried's corpse in the middle.)

BRÜNNHILDE.

> O, er war rein! —
> Treuer als von ihm
> wurden Eide nie gewahrt:
> dem Freunde treu, von der eig'nen Trauten
> schied er sich durch sein Schwert. —
> Hab' Dank nun, Hagen!
> Wie ich dich hieß,
> wo ich dich's wies,
> hast du für Wotan
> ihn gezeichnet, —
> zu dem ich nun mit ihm ziehe. —
> Nun tragt mir Scheite, zu schichten den Haufen
> am Uferrande des Rhein's:
> hoch lod're der Brand, *der den edlen Leib*
> *des* herrlichsten *Helden verzehre!*
> *Sein Roß führet daher,*
> *daß mit mir dem Recken es folge:*
> *denn zu des Helden heiligster Ehre*
> den Göttern erleg' ich den eig'nen Leib.
> *Vollbringet Brünnhild's* letzte Bitte!

(Die Mannen errichten am Ufer einen mächtigen Scheithaufen: Frauen schmücken ihn mit Decken, Kräutern und Blumen.)

BRÜNNHILDE.

> *Mein Erbe nehm' ich nun zu eigen.*

(Sie nimmt den Ring von Siegfried's Finger, steckt ihn sich an und betrachtet ihn mit tiefem Sinnen.)

> Du übermuthiger Held,
> wie hieltest du mich gebannt!
> All' meiner Weisheit mußt' ich entrathen,
> denn all' mein Wissen verrieth ich dir:
> was du mir nahmst, nütztest du nicht, —
> deinem muthigen Trotz vertrautest du nur!
> Nun du, gefriedet, frei es mir gabst,
> kehrt mir mein Wissen wieder,
> erkenn' ich des Ringes Runen.
> Der Nornen Rath vernehm' ich nun auch,
> darf ihren Spruch jetzt deuten:
> des kühnsten Mannes mächtigste That,
> mein Wissen taugt sie zu weih'n. —

BRÜNNHILDE

> O, he was pure! —
> No one ever held oaths
> More truly than he:
> True to his friend, from his own beloved
> He separated himself with his sword —
> Have my thanks, Hagen!
> As I ordered you,
> As I showed you,
> You have marked him
> Now for Wotan. —
> To whom I now take him —
> Now bring me logs to build the pyre
> Here on the banks of the Rhine:
> Let the fire burn high that will devour the corpse
> Of the most magnificent hero of all!
> Lead his steed here.
> So that it can accompany with me the warrior:
> For to the hero's highest honor
> I offer my own body as sacrifice.
> Carry out Brünnhilde's last wish!

(The vassals build a mighty funeral pyre on the banks: women decorate it with blankets, herbs, and flowers.)

BRÜNNHILDE

> I take now my inheritance in possession.

(She takes the ring from Siegfried's finger, puts it on her own and looks at it in deep thought.)

> You proudest hero,
> How you held me in your spell!
> I had to give up all my wisdom,
> For I gave all my wisdom to you:
> What you took from me, you did not use —
> You only trusted your courageous spirit!
> Now you, brought to peace, give it back freely,
> My wisdom returns to me again,
> I recognize the ring's runes.
> I also understand the Norn's counsel,
> I can interpret their speech:
> The mightiest deed of the boldest man,
> My wisdom is able to bless it —

Ihr Nibelungen, vernehmt mein Wort!
eure Knechtschaft künd' ich auf:
der den Ring geschmiedet, euch Rührige band, —
nicht soll er ihn wieder empfah'n, —
doch frei sei er, wie ihr!
Denn dieses Gold gebe ich euch,
weise Schwestern der Wassertiefe!
Das Feuer, das mich verbrennt,
rein'ge den Ring vom Fluch:
ihr löset ihn auf und lauter bewahrt
das strahlende *Gold* des Rhein's,
das zum Unheil euch geraubt! —
Nur einer herrsche:
Allvater! Herrlicher du!
Freue dich des freiesten Helden!
Siegfried führ' ich dir zu:
biet' ihm minnlichen Gruß,
dem Bürgen ewiger Macht!

(Der Scheithaufen ist bereits in Brand gesteckt; das Roß ist Brünnhilde zugeführt: sie faßt es beim Zaum, küßt es und raunt ihm mit leiser Stimme in's Ohr:)

Freue dich, Grane: bald sind wir frei!

(Auf ihr Geheiß tragen die Mannen Siegfried's Leiche in feierlichem Zuge auf den Holzstoß: Brünnhilde folgt ihr zunächst mit dem Rosse, das sie am Zaume geleitet; hinter der Leiche besteigt sie dann mit ihm den Scheithaufen.)

DIE FRAUEN.
(zur Seite stehend, während die Mannen Siegfried's Leiche erheben und dann im Umzuge geleiten.)
Wer ist der Held, den ihr erhebt,
wo führt ihr ihn feierlich hin?
DIE MANNEN.
Siegfried, den Held, erheben wir,
führen zum Feuer ihn hin.
DIE FRAUEN.
Fiel er im Streit? Starb er im Haus?
Geht er nach Hellja's Hof?
DIE MANNEN.
Der ihn erschlug, besiegte ihn nicht,
nach Walhall wandert der Held.

Nibelungs, hear my word!
Your slavery is now ended:
The one who forged the ring and bound you diligent workers,
He will not receive it back —
But let him be free, as you are!
For I give this gold to you
Wise sisters of the water's depths.
The fire, that burns my body
Will cleanse the ring of its curse:
You will melt it down and protect it,
The pure, radiant gold of the Rhine,
Which was stolen from you to great misfortune! —
Let only one rule:
All-father! Magnificent one!
Rejoice in the freest of heroes!
Siegfried I bring to you:
Give him a loving greeting,
The protector of eternal power!

(The pyre has been set alight, the steed has been led to Brünnhilde: she takes the reins, kisses it and whispers with a soft voice into its ear:)

Rejoice Grane, soon we shall be free!

(At her command the vassals carry Siegfried's corpse in a solemn procession to the pyre: Brünnhilde follows immediately behind with the horse, which she leads by the bridle. Behind the corpse she ascends the pyre.)

THE WOMEN
(standing aside, while the men lift Siegfried's corpse and then accompany it in procession)
> Who is the hero, whom you raise,
> Where are you taking him so solemnly?

THE VASSALS
> Siegfried, the hero, we raise
> We bring him to the pyre.

THE WOMEN
> Did he fall in battle? Did he die at home?
> Is he going to Hellja's court?

THE VASSALS
> The one who killed him did not conquer him,
> The hero goes now to Valhalla.

DIE FRAUEN.
> Wer folgt ihm nach, daß nicht auf die Ferse
> Walhall's Thüre ihm fällt?

DIE MANNEN.
> Ihm folgt sein Weib in den Weihebrand,
> ihm folgt sein rüstiges Roß.

DIE MANNEN und FRAUEN ZUSAMMEN.
(nachdem die letzteren sich dem Zuge angeschlossen.)
> Wotan! Wotan! Waltender Gott!
> Wotan, weihe den Brand!
> Brenne Held und Braut,
> brenne das treue Roß:
> daß wundenheil und rein,
> Allvater's freie Genossen,
> Walhall froh sie begrüßen
> zu ewiger Wonne vereint!

(Die Flammen sind hoch über den Opfern zusammengeschlagen, so daß diese dem Blick bereits gänzlich entschwunden sind. In dem ganz finsteren Vordergrunde erscheint Alberich hinter Hagen.)

ALBERICH.
(nach dem Vordergrunde deutend.)
> Mein Rächer, Hagen, mein Sohn!
> Rette, rette den Ring!

Hagen wendet sich rasch und wirft, bereit sich in die Lohe zu stürzen, Speer und Schild von sich. Plötzlich leuchtet aus der Gluth ein blendend heller Glanz auf: auf düst'rem Wolkensaume [gleichsam dem Dampfe des erstickten Holzfeuers] erhebt sich der Glanz, in welche man Brünnhilde erblickt, wie sie, behelmt und in strahlendem Waffenschmucke, auf leuchtendem Rosse, als Walküre, Siegfried an der Hand durch die Lüfte geleitet. Zugleich und während sich die Wolke hebt, schwellen unter ihr die Uferwellen des Rheines bis zur Halle an: die drei Wasserfrauen, vom hellsten Mondlichte beleuchtet, entführen, von den Wellen getragen, den Ring und den Tarnhelm: — Hagen stürzt wie wahnsinnig auf sie zu, das Kleinod ihnen zu entreißen: die Frauen erfassen ihn und ziehen ihn mit sich in die Tiefe hinab. Alberich versinkt mit wehklagender Gebärde.

Der Vorhang fällt.

Ende

THE WOMEN
>Who follows him, so that Valhalla's doors
>Do not strike him on the heels?

THE VASSALS
>His wife follows him to the sacrificial fire,
>His mighty steed follows him.

THE VASSALS and the WOMEN TOGETHER
(after the latter have joined the procession)
>Wotan! Wotan! Ruling god!
>Wotan, bless the pyre!
>Burn hero and bride,
>Burn the faithful steed:
>So that free of wounds and pure,
>All-father's free companions,
>Valhalla can greet them
>United in eternal bliss!

(The flames come together high over the victims so that they disappear completely from view. In the darkest foreground Alberich appears behind Hagen.)

ALBERICH
(pointing toward the foreground)
>My avenger, Hagen, my son!
>Save it, Save the ring!

(Hagen turns quickly and throws aside spear and shield in readiness to leap into the flames. Suddenly there comes from the fire a blindingly bright light: On a dark bank of clouds [as from the ashes of a doused wood fire] there appears the light in which one can see Brünnhilde, as she — in helmet, radiant armor, and on a brilliant steed, as a Valkyrie — leads Siegfried by the hand through the air. At the same time as the cloud lifts, the waves along the Rhine's bank swell up to the hall and the three waterwomen, lighted by the brightest moonlight, carry away the ring and the Tarnhelm: Hagen throws himself at them like a madman in an attempt to wrest the ring from them: The women seize him and drag him into the depths. Alberich sinks down with a lamenting gesture.)

The curtain falls.

The End

Commentary on the Transition from
Siegfried's Tod to *Götterdämmerung*

Prologue and First Act

THE PROLOGUE OF *Siegfried's Tod* consists of two scenes: the Norn scene, which takes place within sight of Brünnhilde's rock, and the farewell scene between Siegfried and Brünnhilde. Although the Norn scene seems to occupy the same place and fulfill essentially the same role of drawing attention to Siegfried's deeds and his death as it does in *Götterdämmerung*, in *Siegfried's Tod* it refers only to those events Wagner considered important for this drama. In fact, there is only a single line from this original text that survives into *Götterdämmerung*. The Norse sources mention three names for the Norns: Urð, Verðandi, and Skuld.[1] The names refer transparently to the past, the present, and the future. Wagner retains the implied roles of the three, but he does not give them names, calling them simply the First, Second, and Third Norns. They tell us that Alberich had stolen the gold and made the ring, which the gods stole in order to pay for their castle. There is no mention of the downfall of the gods or the end of "fate" that is suggested when the rope of the Norns breaks in *Götterdämmerung*, since these are ideas that occurred later in the composition of the cycle.

The second scene of the prologue in *Siegfried's Tod*, the duet between Siegfried and Brünnhilde, on the other hand, has been transferred to the final text of *Götterdämmerung* almost verbatim. Only slight stylistic changes affect a few lines, but the conclusion of the scene is revised to reduce the role of the gods.

The first act proper is broken into several scenes, but it has two settings: the Hall of the Gibichungs and Brünnhilde's rock, the latter of which we have already seen in the prologue. The scene at the hall of the Gibichungs also undergoes little change from version to version. Only the retelling of Siegfried's conception and birth is shortened, since the completed *Ring* has two whole operas devoted to those events. Later, the reference to Siegfried's trip to take revenge on Hunding and his clan for the murder of his father Siegmund is

---

[1] These names appear both in the *Völuspá* and Snorri's *Edda*. Wagner probably derived his Norns from Jacob Grimm's *Deutsche Mythologie*, 4th edition, vol. 1 (Berlin, 1878), 335.

eliminated, since Wagner had dropped it from Siegfried's biography. The only other major change in this scene is to the text of the oath, which is altered to deemphasize the role of the gods in hallowing and avenging the oath. This tendency of Wagner to reduce the role of the gods is evident throughout, though they are still referred to many times, both individually and as a group.

The scene on Brünnhilde's rock with the full group of Valkyries plays an entirely different role in *Siegfried's Tod* than does the scene with Waltraute that replaces it in *Götterdämmerung*. The only thing the two scenes have in common is the contact between the exiled Brünnhilde and the world of the immortal gods. The Valkyries' main concern in *Siegfried's Tod* is to retell Brünnhilde's crime and the punishment Wotan had given her and to establish her opposition to the old world she has left behind. The scene is vastly improved in *Götterdämmerung,* since it allows a deeper understanding of Brünnhilde's love for Siegfried and the situation into which the finale will take us. Waltraute, who has remained a Valkyrie, also represents what Brünnhilde had been, allowing a sort of dialog between the past and the present.

The final scene, with its non-sexual rape, retains its essential shape in *Götterdämmerung*, but Siegfried doesn't tell as many lies in the later version than in *Siegfried's Tod*. In fact, Wagner rewrote the scene so that Siegfried's prevarications are generally true on a literal level. After introducing himself as a Gibichung, something he may consider himself to be after the oath of blood-brotherhood with Gunther, he refers to "himself" in the third person as Gunther. Wagner eliminates the accusation that Brünnhilde's behavior has frightened men. This may have been a slight echo of Siegfried's claim in the *Nibelungenlied* that women would become uppity if they were allowed to make claims like Kriemhild's without being punished. The reference to Siegfried being down at the boat "practicing merry melodies" is also eliminated.

Second Act

Like the Norn scene in the prologue, the scene between Hagen and Alberich seems the same in both versions, but they actually have only a few lines in common. The opening and closing are very similar, but the main content of the version in *Siegfried's Tod* is once again an exposition of events that are more effectively told in the operas conceived and written later. The version in *Götterdämmerung* focuses on Alberich's attitude toward the ring and what Hagen has to do to recover it. The scene is highly effective on the stage, and Wagner was understandably reluctant to jettison it. It is hard to imagine a scene that better shows Hagen's connection to the otherworldly.

The scene of Siegfried's arrival and Hagen's summoning of the vassals is virtually unchanged from *Siegfried's Tod* to *Götterdämmerung*, as is the following scene of Brünnhilde's arrival with Gunther and her accusation of Siegfried. Only the text of the two oaths has been changed to move their

emphasis from the power of the gods to the power of the weapons. The conclusion of each oath is identical.

The "vengeance trio" involving Brünnhilde, Hagen, and Gunther in *Götterdämmerung* is taken over virtually unchanged from *Siegfried's Tod,* although a few words have been added here and there and a second stanza has been added to the trio itself. What has changed radically is what comes after the vengeance trio. In *Siegfried's Tod* the wedding participants return from their visit to the sacrificial altar with Brünnhilde and Gunther pretending to be reconciled. This little passage also contains Siegfried's attempted explanation that the Tarnhelm had only half-covered him. Wagner felt that he needed this, so in the final version of *Götterdämmerung* he moved it into the confusion immediately following the oath and before Siegfried and Gutrune's exit. Here and at the end of the opera Wagner realized that less is more and eliminated a scene that would have been anticlimactic if it had been retained in favor of a highly effective moment carried by the orchestra alone.

Third Act

The song of the Rhine daughters has been retained in *Götterdämmerung* without change. The remainder of the scene is unchanged through all of the versions until the part of the confrontation in which Siegfried refers to the final battle of the gods. Since in *Götterdämmerung* they no longer have a final battle, this passage had to be dropped. Instead, Siegfried says that he has shattered the spear and the rope, the symbols of the eternal law, and that he would have given the ring in exchange for love, but not to save himself. He concludes his confrontation with the Rhine daughters in both versions by symbolically throwing his life away with a clod of dirt.

The second scene proceeds relatively unchanged until we get to Siegfried's narrative. In *Siegfried's Tod* Wagner starts with the line "Mime hieß ein mannlicher Zwerg," which, one is left to assume, means that Mime is in human form. Wagner's idiosyncratic use here of the Middle High German spelling "mannlich," without umlaut, which in its day meant "heroic, manly" (as opposed to the related modern word "männlich," with umlaut, meaning "male, masculine") makes translation confounding, because he goes to great lengths to show that the dwarf is not manly. In *Götterdämmerung*, Wagner resolves the problem by using the word "mürrisch" (bad-tempered) instead of "mannlich." There also, the entire narrative has been changed to reflect the changed plot in *Siegfried* and the fact that Siegfried no longer has to deal with Hunding and his sons. Two brief passages having to do with the dragon's blood, the forest bird (which becomes singular in the revision), and the warning about Mime are retained without much change, although they are separated in the revision. The sequence of instructions by the forest bird is also changed. Here Siegfried is first instructed to kill Mime and then he is told about the ring and

Tarnhelm. The narration of the finding and awakening of Brünnhilde are retained almost verbatim until just before the actual murder. In *Siegfried's Tod* Hagen says that the ravens are setting out to announce Siegfried to Wotan, while in the revision — with its playing down of the gods' role — Hagen says that they are advising him to carry out vengeance. Siegfried's final speech in *Siegfried's Tod* addresses Brünnhilde as a Valkyrie, a role she will now return to in order to lead him to Valhalla, whereas *Götterdämmerung* has a much more intimate vision of a reawakening of Brünnhilde that perhaps parallels her recovery of her senses after Siegfried's death.

The lonely little scene with Gudrune/Gutrune is retained with only a couple of words changed. The portion of the following scene from *Siegfried's Tod* up until Brünnhilde's entrance is also retained. Brünnhilde's final speech, on the other hand, has been rewritten almost entirely. The few lines retained here have to do with the fire purging the ring of its curse. Much has been written about the different versions of Brünnhilde's final speech, and the published version of the libretto of *Götterdämmerung* even includes a passage that Wagner did not set, with the explanation in a footnote that the music has taken over the role of these words.[2] In *Siegfried's Tod* Wagner has the vassals and the ladies of the court sing a chorus over the slain Siegfried as they bear the body to the pyre. In *Götterdämmerung,* Wagner wisely chose to eliminate this anticlimactic passage and to turn the final moments over to the orchestra, as he had done in the second act. Hagen's outcry as the Rhine daughters carry away the ring is an echo of Alberich's final exhortation to his son in *Siegfried's Tod*. This conclusion lets Hagen have the last words in the entire *Ring,* but they are followed immediately by his death. Many observers (and some stage directors) have reminded us that Alberich is still alive, a fact that is emphasized in *Siegfried's Tod* by having him on stage at the end, so that evil is not gone from the world, although it is unclear what he would do without the ring.

In one respect, however, this original version of the death of Siegfried is not as enigmatic as that portrayed in *Götterdämmerung*. Returning to her original role as a Valkyrie, Brünnhilde leads Siegfried to his rightful place among the heroes of Valhalla. In the final version of the *Ring,* neither Siegfried nor his father accepts the Valkyrie's offer of eternal bliss among the gods, but in *Siegfried's Tod* the final scene leaves no doubt about the outcome. "On a dark bank of clouds [as from the ashes of a doused wood fire] there appears the light in which one can see Brünnhilde, as she — in helmet, radiant armor, and on a brilliant steed, as a Valkyrie — leads Siegfried by the hand through the air." This scene is presaged by Siegfried's vision at his moment of death. In

---

[2] Stewart Spencer has brought together the various concluding texts from *Siegfried's Tod* to *Götterdämmerung* in his translation included in *Wagner's Ring of the Nibelung: A Companion,* ed. Stewart Spencer and Barry Millington (New York: Thames and Hudson, 1993), 360–63.

Siegfried's Tod Wagner saw Siegfried's sacrifice as the necessary means to return the gods to power, but in the final version of the *Ring,* Siegfried's death marks the end of the gods' power.

Further Reading

Works by Richard Wagner

My Life. Trans. Andrew Gray, ed. Mary Whittall. Cambridge: Cambridge UP, 1983.

Der Ring des Nibelungen. This is a critical edition in progress, with one volume devoted to each single act. Mainz: B. Schott's Söhne, 1980–. The individual volumes are as follows: *Das Rheingold*, ed. Egon Voss, vol. 1, 1988; vol. 2, 1989; *Die Walküre*, ed. Christa Jost, vol. 1, 2002; vol. 2, 2004; vol. 3, 2005. *Siegfried*, ed. Klaus Döge, vol. 1, 2006; vol. 2, 2008; vol. 3 not yet published); *Götterdämmerung*, ed. Hartmut Fladt, vol. 1, 1981; vol. 2, 1980; vol. 3, 1982. Each volume also contains an essay and a critical report on the revisions made. A volume of documents related to the *Ring* cycle, edited by Werner Breig and Hartmut Fladt, was published in the same series in 1976. It was optimistically labeled *Dokumente I*, but no second volume has appeared.

Sämtliche Schriften und Dichtungen. 16 vols. Leipzig: Breitkopf und Härtel, n.d. [1911].

Stories and Essays. Ed. Charles Osborne. LaSalle, IL: Open Court, 1973. Contains translations of an interesting assortment, including *Die Wibelungen* and the infamous *Das Judentum in der Musik*.

English Translations of Major Sources of the *Ring*

The Nibelungenlied. Trans. A. T. Hatto. London: Penguin, 1965. This is a prose translation with an excellent afterword.

Das Nibelungenlied: Song of the Nibelungs. Trans. Burton Raffel. New Haven: Yale UP, 2006. A verse translation.

The Poetic Edda. Trans. Carolyne Larrington. Oxford: Oxford UP, 1996.

The Saga of Thidrek of Bern. Trans. Edward R. Haymes. New York: Garland, 1988.

The Saga of the Volsungs. Trans. Jesse Byock. London: Penguin,

Sturluson, Snorri. *Edda*. Trans. Anthony Faulkes. London: Dent, 1987.

Secondary Literature

Bailey, Robert. "Wagner's Musical Sketches for *Siegfrieds Tod*." In *Studies in Music History: Essays for Oliver Strunk*, ed. Harold Powers, 459–94. Princeton, NJ: Princeton UP, 1968.

Bermbach, Udo. *Der Wahn des Gesamtkunstwerks: Richard Wagners politisch-ästhetische Utopie*. Frankfurt am Main: Fischer, 1994. An extremely cogent examination of Wagner's views in the light of nineteenth-century philosophy and political thought. Unfortunately not available in translation.

Berry, Mark. *Treacherous Bonds and Laughing Fire: Politics and Religion in Wagner's* Ring. Aldershot: Ashgate, 2006. Takes up some of the points raised by Bermbach, but is far more musicologically oriented.

Björnsson, Árni. *Wagner and the Volsungs: Icelandic Sources of* Der Ring des Nibelungen. Trans. Anthony Faulkes and Anna Yates. London: Viking Society for Northern Research, 2003.

Borchmeyer, Dieter. *Drama and the World of Richard Wagner*. Trans. Daphne Ellis. Princeton, NJ: Princeton UP, 2003. German original: *Richard Wagner: Ahasvers Wandlungen*. Frankfurt am Main and Leipzig: Insel, 2002.

Buller, Jeffrey L. *Classically Romantic: Classical Form and Meaning in Wagner's* Ring. n.p.: Xlibris, 2001.

Cooke, Deryck. *I Saw the World End: A Study of Wagner's* Ring. Oxford: Oxford UP, 1979. A valuable study, unfortunately truncated by the author's death.

Darcy, Warren. *Wagner's* Das Rheingold. Oxford: Clarendon Press, 1993. One of the most thorough explorations of the *Ring's* beginnings in English.

Deathridge, John, Martin Geck, and Egon Voss. *Wagner Werk-Verzeichnis (WWV)*. Mainz: Schott, 1986. Provides reliable information on the dating, provenance, and location of manuscripts and editions of the musical works. The works translated in the present volume are treated in the *WWV* as preliminary material to Götterdämmerung.

Gregor-Dellin, Martin. *Richard Wagner: Sein Leben, Sein Werk, Sein Jahrhundert*. Munich: Goldmann, 1983. In English (abridged) *Richard Wagner: His Life, His Work, His Century*. Trans. J. Maxwell Brownjohn. San Diego, New York, London: Harcourt Brace Jovanovich, 1983. A comprehensive biography of the composer. Particularly useful for its use of independent sources to fill in facts about Wagner's life the composer suppressed or left out when he wrote his autobiographies.

Hauer, Stanley R. "Wagner and the 'Völospá.'" *19th Century Music* 15(1991): 32–43.

Kitcher, Philip, and Richard Schacht. *Finding an Ending: Reflections on Wagner's* Ring. Oxford: Oxford UP, 2004.

Lee, M. Owen. *Athena Sings: Wagner and the Greeks.* Toronto: U of Toronto P, 2003.

Magee, Elizabeth. *Richard Wagner and the Nibelungs.* Oxford: Clarendon Press, 1990.

Millington, Barry. *The New Grove: Wagner.* London: Macmillan, 2002.

Millington, Barry. *Wagner.* Revised edition. Princeton, NJ: Princeton UP, 1992. A solid and readable overview of the composer's life and works.

Newman, Ernest. *The Wagner Operas.* Princeton, NJ: Princeton UP, 1991.

Spencer, Stewart, and Barry Millington, eds. *Wagner's Ring of the Nibelung: A Companion.* London: Thames and Hudson, 1993. Contains an excellent translation of the *Ring* by Spencer, including all the versions of Brünnhilde's final scene.

Strobel, Otto. *Skizzen und Entwürfe zur Ring-Dichtung: Mit der Dichtung "Der junge Siegfried."* Munich: Bruckmann, 1930.

Index

Note: Entries for characters and events within the texts and translations have been omitted.